COMING FROM TH

Quaker Peacebuilding Initiatives in
Northern Ireland
1969-2007

COMING FROM THE SILENCE

Quaker Peacebuilding Initiatives
in Northern Ireland
1969-2007

Editors Ann Le Mare and Felicity McCartney

Quaker Service, Belfast

ISBN 978-0-9568203-0-3

First published in 2009 by
William Sessions Limited,
York, England.

This edition published in 2011 by
Quaker Service
541 Lisburn Road
Belfast BT9 7GQ

This edition designed by April Sky Design, Newtownards
www.aprilsky.co.uk
and printed by GPS Colour Graphics Ltd, Belfast

CONTENTS

ACKNOWLEDGEMENTS

THE COMMITTEE of Quaker House Belfast decided to write a history of their project and Ulster Quaker Service wanted to record their work as their 40th anniversary loomed. A friend from the Irish School of Ecumenics challenged one of the editors, 'Why doesn't somebody write up what the Friends did during the Troubles in Northern Ireland?' David Bass had all the records from the Centre for Neighbourhood Development and Jo Noble had those of the Quaker Peace Education Project. So the different interests came together in an editorial committee which met several times over a year and a half and set this publication in motion. The editors appreciate all the work that went into it from authors and editorial committee in 2008-9. We hope the book will be useful for those interested in Quakers, or in faith-based social action, for students and practitioners of conflict resolution and for anybody interested in modern Irish studies.

Thanks are due also to Stephen Pittam for the Preface and to Clem McCartney for the Conclusions. Joyce Neill and Alastair Reid helped us by reading drafts of various chapters. The editors also want to thank Katy Cullinan and Janet Mickevich for proofreading and Chris McCartney and Jonathan Le Mare for help with diagrams. Libraries at Northern Ireland Community Relations Council in Belfast, Irish School of Ecumenics, Dublin and Woodbrooke Quaker Study Centre, Birmingham were helpful in making material available. Jo Noble and Rosemary Fulton collected and typed material and David Bass, Jo Noble and Janette McKnight collated the photo plates. Philip McDonagh, Janet Pritchard and Felicity McCartney formed a fundraising subcommittee and successful applications were made to the Joseph Rowntree Charitable Trust and the Robert and Kezia Chapman Trust to whom we are very grateful.

Many Quakers gave us their reminiscences of the work that went on and contributed photographs, but most of all, we thank the committee members, volunteers, staff and users of the various projects, the Friends in meetings and others who supported the work over the years and who did not give up even when times were hard. We hope you recognise yourselves in this book and the part you played, large or small.

Ann Le Mare and Felicity McCartney, Editors

Editorial Committee: David Bass, Anne Bennett, Vincent Bent, Roy Blair, Arthur Chapman, Seamus Farrell, Rosemary Fulton, Ann Le Mare, Felicity McCartney, Philip McDonagh, Janette McKnight, Jo Noble, Janet Pritchard.

Cover: Mosaic by Quaker Cottage Teenage Project.

PREFACE

I LIVE IN Yorkshire and I sometimes wonder how Friends in Yorkshire would have responded to a conflict like 'the Troubles'. After all, Yorkshire is an area about the same size as Northern Ireland and there are probably twice as many Quakers living in the region. Would we have dug deep into our tradition to find unique ways to respond to the humanitarian crisis? Would our long-standing concerns for those in prison lead us to find new ways to respond to the needs of families of those incarcerated? Would the conflict lead us to explore innovative ideas for showing the value of our peace testimony?

Thankfully, Yorkshire Friends have not been tested in this way. Ulster Friends have. This book is testimony to the magnificent way in which they have responded, in different ways and over such a long period of time.

Three themes stand out for me as I reflect on the different chapters and ponder on my own engagement with Quaker work in Northern Ireland, as a young volunteer in the 1970s and more recently through my role as a funder with the Joseph Rowntree Charitable Trust.

First, is the inspiration that comes from individuals taking forward their deeply felt Quaker concerns. So much of Quaker service in Northern Ireland has developed because of wise people who have been driven by what Mike Yarrow describes as the 'religiously inspired impulse to action'*. The Society of Friends has developed creative ways for testing these concerns to build a wider ownership of the work, but at its best the Society provides a marvellous vehicle for inspired individuals to draw on their experiences and to act on their convictions.

---

* Mike Yarrow, *Quaker Experiences in International Conciliation,* Yale University Press, page 261.

Second, is the variety of the work that these case studies show. The Spirit leads us to act in different ways. For some offering a service to those in prison or to families under stress is what they feel called to do. For others exploring how schools can become more peaceful places is a priority. Addressing the conflict by tackling the underlying issues of poverty and injustice led some to a community development strategy. Finding ways to support agreement and reconciliation at a political level is the priority for others. All of the different approaches are important and are connected. For Quakers social change looks more like a patchwork than a linear process.

Third, is the spirit in which the work has been undertaken, and the unifying values that underpin it. The fundamental belief of that of God in all people has led Quakers to bear witness for equality, justice, reconciliation and peace throughout the world. It is these values that underpin all the work described here. The values are shared by others within all denominations and faiths and those of none, as is witnessed by the fact that some work has been undertaken jointly and some handed on for others to take forward. In this instance Friends have drawn on their values and have felt well placed and a particular imperative to initiate action.

It is a good time to publish this book. Thankfully, the peace process, to which all these initiatives contributed has brought Northern Ireland to a very different place. The work is not finished and there remains much to do to address the legacy of 'the Troubles'. However, the radically changed context makes it appropriate to publish this carefully prepared record of how the small Quaker community in Northern Ireland initiated such a range of creative responses to the conflict and its underlying causes. There is a lot to learn from this study and so much to celebrate.

Stephen Pittam
Trust Secretary
The Joseph Rowntree Charitable Trust
June 2009

AUTHORS' PROFILES

DAVID BASS

David (also known as Fred) was born in 1948 in Lisburn, where he attended the Quaker Meeting and Friends School. In 1969 he worked with Felicity McKerr (now McCartney) to establish Irish Quaker Work Camps, and was one of the leaders on the first two Ballymurphy Play Schemes in 1970 and 1971. In 1974 he became a member of the original committee for Centre for Neighbourhood Development, maintaining his involvement in various roles including Convenor, until it closed in 1992. He served as a Board Member for the Ashton Centre Project in New Lodge, Belfast, which had its origins in CfND. In 1991 he joined the Ulster Quaker Service Committee and is now a Board Member of Quaker Service, serving as Treasurer.

David is married, with three grown up children and lives in Belfast. He recently retired from the Northern Ireland Housing Executive where he worked for over thirty years.

ANNE BENNETT

Anne was born in England but has a long association with Northern Ireland. She lectured at Queen's University, Belfast and was an active member of the Ulster Quaker Service Committee for a number of years. She left to work full time for Quakers in London being involved with the work at the United Nations and later, peace making and peace building programmes in areas of conflict. After taking early retirement, she worked for Quakers in Lebanon and then returned to Belfast when she was appointed as the Representative at Quaker House, where she worked from August 2004 - May 2007. Although she is now based in England near her two daughters and grandchildren, she continues her active links with Quaker House.

ROY BLAIR

Roy has been a Friend since 1973 and a member of Frederick Street Meeting since 1976. With a social work background he has had continuous involvement with Quaker Service since 1979. Roy became the Chairman in 2005.

ARTHUR CHAPMAN

Arthur was born in 1928 in Portadown. He studied at Queens University Belfast, and graduated in French and German. He married Dr. Alice Davis and is now widowed 30 years with 4 grown up children, living in Scotland and Northern Ireland. Arthur is a lifelong Ulster Quaker who worked in various schools in Northern Ireland, including Headship of Friends' School, Lisburn from 1970-1989. He has been Clerk of Ulster QM and Assistant Clerk of Ireland Yearly Meeting. Arthur is currently a member of Portadown Friends Meeting, but living in Lisburn.

SEAMUS FARRELL

Seamus was born in Co. Derry in 1944 and currently lives in Londonderry/Derry, where he is engaged in the development of training for facilitators of "Towards Understanding and Healing" workshops for those who have been affected by conflict in Ireland and abroad. He spent 25 years in overseas development work in Africa: was engaged for 2 years in Bosnia Herzegovina , supporting schools' efforts to contribute to social cohesion: during 2002 directed training in Nigeria for individuals and agencies engaging with ethnic and religious conflict. Seamus spent 10 years with QPEP and EMUpsp in the development of conflict management skills training for schools, and has also been involved in mediation in the context of the conflict in Northern Ireland. He continues this work and has been developing Peer Mediation in schools in Tallagh, Ballymun and Blanchardstown, Dublin, as well as progressing the concept of Peer Mediation at in-service professional development level for post-primary children with Secondary Teachers throughout the Republic of Ireland.

ANN LE MARE

Ann, an American Friend, (also known as Lisa (nee) Huber) came to Belfast in the summer of 1972 to be a leader on the Irish Quaker

Work Camps in Ballymurphy. Subsequently she was employed as a community development worker in East Belfast by the Community Relations Commission, and then as the development worker with CfND. Recently, she was on the Management Committee of Quaker House for 9 years. Ann is married with three grown up children and lives in Kendal. She has worked for the Open University for many years, and is currently a lecturer in human geography and development at Durham University.

CLEM McCARTNEY

Clem has been a free lance consultant on conflict and community issues for 17 years. He has been involved informally with Quaker service work in Northern Ireland since the beginning of the 1970s, and with British Friends international work for 20 years. Clem is an attender at Coleraine Meeting.

FELICITY McCARTNEY

Felicity, (formerly McKerr) from Lurgan, was active in the Belfast work camps as a Young Friend and went on to work in Youth Work and Community Development in the NICRC and Centre for Neighbourhood Development, before taking an MA in Adult and Continuing Education. Later she worked in Limavady Community Development Initiative and then for the Community Foundation for Northern Ireland until her retirement in 2005. She was involved in several of the projects described in this book.

ILLUSTRATIONS

Chapter 1

INTRODUCTION – LOOKING BEHIND THE QUAKER WORK

Felicity McCartney

*'True godliness don't turn men out of the world,
but enables them to live better in it and excites their
endeavours to mend it; not hide their candle under
a bushel, but set it upon a table in a candlestick'.*
William Penn 1682 (QFP 21.17)

THIS INTRODUCTION aims to show how the work in Northern Ireland came from both a commitment to 'Faith in Action' and a Quaker tradition of relief and peace work. Although motivated by spiritual concern, Friends* often work with others, as will be seen in Chapters 2-6. This chapter will refer to other Quaker initiatives for peace, justice and equality, to theoretical perspectives and to activity by others in the fields of conflict resolution, community relations, community development, justice and peace.

QUAKER BELIEFS AND VALUES

The Religious Society of Friends, popularly known as Quakers, was founded in England in 1652 by George Fox and spread rapidly to Ireland. The central tenet of Quaker belief is that there is 'that of God'** in every person, leading to a belief both in the

---

* 'Friends' is used here interchangeably with 'Quakers'.
** Also called 'the inward light', 'the Christ within' and other similar descriptions.

importance of individual spiritual experience and of a divine presence in all aspects of life and relationships (Gorman 1981, p.20). The implication of this simple idea is that Faith and Practice are closely connected and that everyday life is an outworking of Faith. Dale explains how faith and action or 'being' and 'doing' are not in opposition to each other and warns Friends to guard against emphasising one to the detriment of the other (Dale 1996, p.20). Spiritual inspiration may come from everyday life just as resolve to action may be clarified in a meeting for worship, if we are open to being guided.

Testimonies and Concerns

Historically, Quakers developed testimonies which are not so much beliefs as convictions leading to action. The peace testimony is the best known of these, but there are also other testimonies for example, to truth (often called integrity), to equality, to simplicity and many others. Punshon captures the breadth of the testimonies when he says:

> '[The Testimonies]...are religious, ethical, collective, demanding, developing—and vague. In fact, the area of imprecision with which they are surrounded is the greatest strength of the testimonies. It enables them to be flexible as circumstances in the world change, and provides individual Friends with a constant challenge to work out for themselves what God is asking of them. ...[T]hey have a strong corporate dimension and theologically reflect the freedom of the gospel against the literalism of the law'.
>
> Punshon, J. 1990 p.19

A concern is an inward calling to carry out a particular service. This would be brought to the meeting by the individual who felt called and may be supported in various ways from moral support for the Friend, to providing finance to release him or her to act, or the setting up of a committee to undertake the service corporately. The progress of a concern is to some extent a process for establishing a piece of work among a wider group of Quakers. Yarrow explains this more fully (Yarrow 1978, p.7).

Much of the work described in this book was undertaken by Friends in response to testimonies and under concern. Indeed much of it originated with a few individuals and was brought to meetings for wider support. In the case of the four charities

2

described in chapters 3-6, this led to the setting up of committees to undertake major work over several years. Two of these, Quaker Service and Quaker House Belfast are still in operation in 2009.

HISTORY

Throughout history Quakers have been known for their activism and philanthropy, as for example, their opposition to the slave trade, famine relief in Ireland, prison reform, industrial philanthropy and the Friends Ambulance Unit which enabled those who would not fight with outward weapons to serve in a medical capacity during wars (Greenwood 1975). But these activities are complemented by a great many small contributions by individuals and groups of Friends responding as well as they could to the ills of the world around them.

Some of the tested methods used by previous Quakers echo in the work that was done in Northern Ireland. The idea of 'speaking truth to power', an early form of lobbying governments and others in authority, is to be found throughout historic writings. In 1827 English Friend Elizabeth Fry together with her brother John Joseph Gurney wrote to the Lord Lieutenant of Ireland 'to preserve the poor from starvation is a duty which appears to devolve not only on the benevolence of individuals, but in case of absolute need, on the justice of the whole community' (Greenwood 1975, p.27). That society has responsibility for welfare is an idea accepted now, but at that time novel. The same J.J. Gurney was later to be found in 1837 putting to the President in Washington that if former slaves could be independent in the West Indies, why couldn't they be free in North America?

The concern for prisoners has its origins in the fact that early Friends were often imprisoned themselves and therefore saw penal conditions at first hand. Conscientious objectors, among them many Friends, continued to be imprisoned in many countries up until the 20th century and some countries still do not have legitimate status for this group. Early Friends often tried to support and comfort fellow prisoners and it was in 19th century that reformer Elizabeth Fry (who recently appeared on the British five pound note) began her campaign to bring comfort, hope and occupation to prisoners, including teaching both sewing and reading. Pricilla Buxton, writing in 1847, is quoted as saying about Elizabeth Fry:

'There was no weakness or trouble of mind that could not be unveiled to [Elizabeth Fry].... She always could see hope for everyone: she invariably found or made some point of light. The most abandoned must have felt she did not despair for them, either for this world or another; and it was this that made her irresistible'.

QFP 23.99

A further concern of Elizabeth Fry was the conditions on prison ships to Australia and she provided women travelling on these with a 'bag of useful things' including material and needles for sewing. This is depicted on panel E6 of the Quaker Tapestry*.

Prisoners of war were another theme for Quakers since the 19th century, further developed by both British and German Friends during the Second World War. This took the form of provision of items such as seeds and tools for gardening, books in the appropriate language and musical instruments. Moral issues to do with conditions in which prisoners were held were also taken up by British Friends, along with churches and other groups, and speedy repatriation supported at the end of the war (Greenwood 1975, p.272). Quaker Council for European Affairs (QCEA) remains involved in collecting information on prison conditions throughout Europe and published a report on women prisoners (QCEA 2007). So the work of Ulster Quaker Service Committee (UQSC) for prisoners and their families in Northern Ireland grew out of a long and continuing tradition of concern for alleviation and change in the conditions in which people are held in custody and for alternative forms of justice.

Providing relief from suffering was seen as a Christian duty, irrespective of the loyalties of the victims. Thus, Friends in Philadelphia in 1774 seeking to raise funds from their Yearly Meeting, said it was to be 'for the relief of the necessitous of every religious denomination' (Greenwood 1975, p.4) and similarly, Irish immigrants in America in the nineteenth century, contributing to famine relief in Ireland 'preferred to use the neutral Quakers rather than the large British and Anglo-Irish Committees which were considered to be tainted with political and religious prejudice' (Greenwood 1975, p.28).

---

* See photo plate 11 and Glossary for reference to the Tapestry.

4

Cecil Woodham-Smith in her book 'The Great Hunger – Ireland 1845-49' notes that in respect of soup kitchens provided by the Society of Friends 'strictest instructions were given …that no preference should be made in the distribution of relief on the grounds of religious persuasion' (Woodham-Smith 1991, p.158). She describes how Quaker travellers provided reliable witnesses of the effects of the famine, especially in Connaught where relief was not at all organised.

The testimony to Equality often involved opposing prevailing public opinion.

> *'The slavery of Africans and their descendants has become so established, by its long continuance, and the forge of custom and education, that many otherwise well minded persons, …have been led thereby to consider the practice not only admissible, but consistent with justice and social order.…'*
>
> Elias Hicks, quoted in Barbour 1985

Hicks went on to say slavery was inconsistent with Christian teaching of individual freedom of soul and conscience and that Friends should oppose it. This was a long and difficult struggle for many Quakers, as some of their members in the southern states of USA had slaves. John Woolman is known as one of the most vociferous campaigners on this issue, and he is said to have often visited Quaker slave owners and challenged them directly. He also wore only unbleached linen as cotton manufacturing and bleaching was done using slave labour, an early example of a trade boycott, and paid for food provided by slave labour (Whitmire 2007).

PEACE AND PACIFISM

The published peace testimony of 1661 was a statement by Quakers in response to the re-establishment of the monarchy of Charles II. It established the idea that war and outward strife were inconsistent with the spirit of Christ. Its origins were both theological, based on the concept of God as being within each person, and biblical ('love your enemies'). A full text is given in Appendix 1. Although the original is often quoted, it is interpreted by each generation according to its time, and has led to many peace initiatives over the years. Yarrow states that the earliest example of a Quaker conciliation initiative is probably that between Indians and colonists in Rhode Island in 1675 (Yarrow 1978, p.12).

Commitment to peace was not seen only as an idea but a testimony that required action. William Penn, a Quaker and founder of Pennsylvania, wrote 'An Essay towards peace in Europe' (1693) which suggested nations regulate their relationships to avoid future wars, an idea which took nearly three centuries to come to fruition! It showed the commitment even then to 'building the institutions of peace' (Gorman 1981) as well as the individual seeking to lead a peaceful life. It was also connected to the approach to relief work. Rufus Jones describes pacifism as not a theory but a way of life with its origins in St. Paul's belief that it was possible to 'overcome evil with good' (Fosdick 1953).

As one of the historic peace churches, Quakers work from a pacifist position, one of several positions which may be taken by peacemakers (Atack 2008, Ch.6). Yarrow considers the strength of the pacifist position for an intermediary in a conflict situation is '...the belief that it is better to suffer than to inflict suffering which is at the heart of the pacifist position, is a disarming and persuasive element' (Yarrow, p.267). Atack analyses the various pacifist perspectives, some based on belief, others contingent on the situation, for example 'Just War' theory and anti-nuclear campaigns, which depend on the circumstances of the conflict or the weapons to be used. Quakers are clearly in the religiously motivated category, along with other historic peace churches, individual philosophers such as Tolstoy and Hindus in the tradition of Ghandi. A distinguishing factor of 'pure' pacifism is that it does not accept a double morality between individual behaviour and political use of armed force (Wight, cited in Atack, p.84).

Criticism of a pacifist approach has included that it does not challenge the state's authority, but can co-exist with a military system, allowing withdrawal as conscientious objectors do in wars. Also that non-violent methods cannot be successfully used to settle international disputes. Quakers have tried at various points in history to challenge the wrongs of society, including those that were state perpetrated, by campaigns of various kinds, not always with positive results. Relief work such as that of the Friends Ambulance Unit (Greenwood 1975, p183) and support of international organisations has enabled Friends to contribute to the opening of communication channels as an alternative to aggressive action.

In Northern Ireland, the various initiatives described in this book were undertaken because of the conflict situation. They were the responses of a peace church to a society which found itself in the middle of political turmoil, street violence, and deep sectarian divisions. The narrative shows meetings with government bodies to try to influence how prisoners and their families were treated, enabling of meetings between opposing politicians, community development and education to build confidence in the most disadvantaged neighbourhoods and in schools and a number of activities which bring people together across the sectarian divide. There were a variety of approaches available to a pacifist group in the situation and these are described in detail in Chapters 2-6 and analysed in Chapters 7 and 8.

SOME 20TH CENTURY DEVELOPMENTS IN QUAKER WORK

Sydney Bailey argues that the response of Quakers to war and peace changed in the 20th century to include reconstruction and to support alternatives to war as a method for solving dispute. The connection between beliefs and action are clearly understood and the link between different types of work, such as relief or service work and political mediation, are also felt to be useful (Bailey 1993). The emphasis on building relationships over the long term rather than short term intervention is to be found in many writings and a complete account of Quaker Relief can be found in 'Quaker Encounters' (Greenwood 1975).

> *'Our task is to abolish war, but in the meantime, it is a proper Quaker activity to reduce the harm that will occur should war break out....'*

Bailey 1993, p.7

Sometimes Friends would have established their credibility through relief or service work before having an opening to influence the powerful, building on a previous Quaker presence, either because there are Quakers living in an area of conflict or because work was done on relief of suffering or other service (Pettigrew 1991).

Another feature of the evolving work was increased cooperation with other organisations such as inter-church bodies, peace and justice groups and the establishment of Non-Governmental

Organisation (NGO) status for Quaker organisations at United Nations (UN) and later the European Union (EU). The projects related in this book show how work inter-relates. For example, the history of prison work at the Maze helped Quaker House to establish contact with the Northern Ireland Office and government generally, as well as with paramilitary groups whose members had been in prison.

Quaker Centres

The concept of Quaker Centres which would work positively for peace was conceived in 1916 and first used, mostly by British and American Friends, for relief work in Europe after the First World War. In the 1920s some closed and others focussed on more general peace making, dealing with refugees and prison work. Later, a centre was to grow in Geneva to relate to first the League of Nations and then at United Nations, gaining NGO status as Quaker United Nations Office (QUNO) and opening another centre in New York (Yarrow 1978, p.29). Activities at the European centres varied and included the promotion of peace, reconciling different cultural groups at times of tension, drawing the attention of leaders to the needs of minorities and reporting human rights violations to the main Quaker organisations to facilitate central lobbying. In the 1930s support for dissidents and Jews became a major activity in Vienna and the German centres, while in Paris the care of refugees, penal reform and drawing attention to the rights of conscience objectors to military service was on the agenda. The Warsaw centre focused on German-Polish relations but was closed down by the authorities in 1929, followed by the Moscow one in 1931. By 1938 four centres remained, in Berlin, Vienna, Paris and Geneva. Small groups of local Friends grew in these countries and work became appropriately localised. German Friends, for example, felt they were less conspicuous as a religious organisation quietly helping minorities, rather than attached to an international Quaker body whose opposition to Nazism would have been noticed by the authorities. (Bailey 1993, p.90).

Conferences for diplomats and international affairs seminars were organised in Europe and USA from 1920s to bring disparate groups together and increase understanding of cultural and political differences. QCEA based at Quaker House Brussels followed with the establishment of the European Economic Community. Quaker House Belfast was in this tradition of Quaker centres. It was established after an exploratory period to see whether there was a role for such a project. The work of other centres was varied, however, and the main objective was to respond to the situation as the representatives found it, as can be seen from the account of Quaker House in Chapter 5.

Modern day Quaker action has yet different manifestations. A glance at the Quaker Peace and Social Witness (QPSW London) web-site shows that they define their role as a 'hub' for national action and exchange of information. The Ecumenical accompanier programme in Israel-Palestine was a QPSW initiative taken up as it grew by the World Council of Churches and administered by Friends on their behalf. A variety of placements and assistant posts intended to enable younger people to get experience of peace work, work on disarmament and peace campaigning are all mentioned and useful tools and links provided for local meetings and others wishing to take their own action. Work in areas of conflict is still being supported, but in a different way with trained staff employed in regions of conflict to work with and support local initiatives. Conciliation teams now carry out the work rather than individual Friends working under concern, as can be seen from the example in Nagaland (Alldred 2007). This move to paid staff is a feature of Quaker work, as it is in many other charities.

QCEA, representative NGO at the European Union, has recently published a study on peacebuilding in the Western Balkans suggesting potential EU intervention in the countries intending to join them (QCEA 1 2009). Another of their concerns is the recognition of the need for conflict prevention in the development programmes of EU in relation to third world countries (QCEA 2 2009). These are sustained examples of work drawing on the grassroots experience of Friends and other peace builders to make recommendations for political action and to monitor whether the good intentions, in this case of EU, are put into practice.

IRELAND

Wigham refers to the work of the Friends Central Relief Committee during the main famine years in 1840s Ireland. They organised a range of relief measures including soup kitchens, distribution of turnip seeds to substitute for the infected potato, recovery of fishermen's nets from pawn and the setting up of a model farm in Co. Galway to experiment with alternative crops (Wigham 1992, pp.84-9). As usual, Quakers kept full documentation of their proceedings and these are a rich detailed record for historians today.

When the latest round of conflict developed in Northern Ireland in 1968, there were 1,600 Quakers in Ireland, almost 800 of whom lived in Northern Ireland. They had a history of humanitarian help to both sides in previous Irish conflicts and of providing unconditional famine relief in the 1840s (Poole 2008).

Local Quaker Denis Barrett was among those already aware of the underlying inequalities when he co-authored 'The Northern Ireland Problem' in 1962 which identified some of the issues later taken up by the Northern Ireland Civil Rights Campaign (Barritt & Carter 1962). So, when trouble broke out in 1968, there was already concern among Friends to try to enable a better society for all.

In 1969 when families were made homeless by attacks on their houses, the Quaker Meeting Houses were among the many buildings used for relief of families in a safe place and the forerunner of Ulster Quaker Service Committee (UQSC) was set up. Later, when internment without trial came in 1971, Quakers set up the visitors' services at the Maze Prison (see Chapter 3). The apparent political stalemate led to preliminary work and then the setting up of Quaker House in 1982 (Chapter 5), another kind of intervention by Friends. Connecting local reconciliation to peaceful settlement of disputes was the theme of the Quaker Peace Education Project (QPEP), which was to work with young people from 1986 to 1994 (Chapter 6), and a different approach again was taken by the Centre for Neighbourhood Development (CfND) (Chapter 4) which supported community development in local neighbourhoods in Belfast as a way of building skills and confidence in deeply divided communities.

All this work was underpinned by the Quaker commitment to faith in action. There was widespread support for these initiatives among British and Irish Friends, and many in Europe, USA and further afield as well as from others as diverse as churches, community groups, peace activists and charitable trusts. Above all, it was actively supported by local Friends and Meetings, many of whom were also involved in their own concerns. Chapter 2 gives a flavour of some of these concerns, covering Young Friends work camps, examples of inter-church and cross community activity and the actions of individuals with support from meetings.

CONFLICT RESOLUTION APPROACHES

Theories of conflict resolution that were developed in the last 30 years, some of which drew on Northern Ireland experience, confirmed some of the features which Quakers had instinctively or spiritually known and incorporated in their activity. For example Lederach's Conflict transformation theory, explained in Chapter 7 Figure 7.1, emphasised the need to build peace at different levels to ensure that any political settlement would be sustainable at grass roots level also. He points out that reconciliation between previously hostile groups is built on the relationships aspects of a conflict and can not rely solely on negotiated settlements, important as these are (Lederach 1997). Further, connections are important between the different levels, so that those at grass roots can have access to both middle level civic society (churches, trade unions, networking bodies and NGOs) and to politicians at the negotiating table and can be empowered to take part in processes to put forward their own views of the future.

Reconciliation based on building good community relations is a major plank of conflict resolution in Northern Ireland, officially recognised by Government in the Community Relations Act of 1969 and central to the work of a number of organisations. Love assesses the value of this approach:

'Most conflict resolution theory assumes that structures can be altered thus changing political relationships. Reconciliation assumes the opposite: that without new trust in human relations and a willingness to forgive and be forgiven, new lasting structures will not emerge. This is especially true where combatants share the same … territory after the 'war' or 'struggle'.

Love 1995

The work undertaken by Quaker House and Ulster Quaker Service Committee (UQSC) reflect these different levels, as they maintained contact with top level decision makers, politicians and officials (level 1), inter-church and peace bodies (level 2), and also

11

local people in areas where there was conflict (level 3), or in the case of UQSC, prisoners and their families. Work in the prison, on interfaces, and through community groups, schools and work camps in local communities helped the various Quaker initiatives to build sound relationships with people in both communities, often the powerless, while participation in networks (churches, restorative justice, voluntary sector and peace networks) in civic society and using contacts helped Quakers to understand the views and policies of politicians and decisions makers (see Chapter 7, Figure 7.1). Much of the recent work of Quaker House has been in the field of reconciliation, strengthening the peace through dialogue and building relationships.

Conflict transformation is one of six theories of peacemaking considered by Ross (2000). It is worth noting that all six are relevant to the Northern Ireland conflict and an analysis of the Quaker projects described in this book shows examples of such activities (see Chapter 7, Figure 7.2). Community relations approaches vary but most involve cross community contact at some point in the exercise, perhaps after a period of separate development. The value of such work is that it enables people to learn about the other side, but Trew warns that this does not always lead to changed attitudes (Trew cited in Love 1995) and asks 'does it always last back home?' The value of work by the major lasting peace organisations, such as the Corrymeela Community, Mediation Northern Ireland or the Peace People, is that it is sustained over a long period and builds peace slowly. The Quaker work is among these, if smaller in scale. The value is also in the links that can be made across organisations.

The Northern Ireland Community Relations Commission (NICRC) established by government in 1970 adopted a community development approach to tackling community relations problems (McCready 2001). Even after the closure of the Commission, this became a widespread strategy for both local government and community organisations. Aimed at empowering local people to take collective action, it was seen as a confidence building measure (ibid). Later the emphasis on the development of local neighbourhoods, mostly consisting of a large majority of Catholics or Protestants, became known as 'single identity work' (Hughes & Donnelly 1997). Some saw a danger in the separate development that this suggested. CfND (Chapter 4) used a community development approach in separate neighbourhoods and made links through central activity. Work camps went into neighbourhoods in support of a community development model, providing a service along with a local tenants' group.

EVALUATING RELIGIOUSLY INSPIRED WORK

Questions of motive often arise when there is intervention in conflict situations, and in the preface to Yarrow's book (1978) Anatol Rapaport offers an answer. He believes that the religiously inspired conviction of the Quakers cannot usefully be analysed on scientific grounds, but the specific methods and techniques of Quaker work can be and need to be subjected to careful scrutiny. He sees this self critical approach in Yarrow's case studies. This view does put a strong responsibility on the support committees for the work to ensure that objective review and evaluation are regularly undertaken, a challenge met by all the major projects described in Chapters 3-6.

CONCLUSIONS

This introduction has covered some of the ideas and philosophies behind the work described in the following chapters. Quaker beliefs and commitment to faith in action has a long and varied history. Pacifism and the peace testimony of Friends is a driving motivation for involvement where conflict and injustice are found. Twentieth century conflict resolution and reconciliation methods have helped us to understand and place this work in a wider context and led naturally to Quakers making alliances. And the practices of reconciliation and community development have underpinned much of the work described. Issues such as professionalisation, the role of volunteers and charitable law reform affected the work, as it did across the voluntary sector. Each of the chapters contains more about the reasons why each particular initiative was taken and why the methods were appropriate. Chapter 7 places the Quaker work in a wider framework and analyses its impact.

References

Alldred, Sarah (2007) 'Quaker Conciliation Work in Nagaland' **The Friend 19 Jan. 2007.**

Atack, Iain **(2005) The Ethics of Peace and War.** Edinburgh: EUP.

Bailey, Sydney D (1993) **Peace Is a Process.** Swathmore Lecture. London: QHS.

Barbour, Hugh (1985) **Slavery and Theology: Writings of Seven Quaker Reformers, 1800-1870.** Dublin (IN): Prinit Press.

Barritt, Denis P & Carter, Charles F (1962) **The Northern Ireland Problem: A Study In Group Relations.** London: Oxford University Press.

Dale, Jonathan (1996) **Beyond the Spirit of the Age.** Swarthmore Lecture. London: Quaker Home Service.

Fosdick, Harry Emerson (1953) **Rufus Jones Speaks to our Time.** London: The Bannisdale Press.

Gorman, George H. (1981) **Introducing Quakers.** London: Quaker Home Service.

Greenwood, John Ormerod (1975) **Quaker Encounters.** York: Sessions.

Hughes, Joanne & Donnelly, Caitlin (1997) **Single Identity Community Relations in Northern Ireland.** School of Public Policy, Economics & Law, University of Ulster at Jordanstown (UUJ).

Love, Mervyn T. (1995) **Peace Building through Reconciliation in Northern Ireland.** Aldershot, England: Avebury; and Brookfield, Vermont: Ashgate.

Lederach, J.P. (1997) **Building Peace: Sustainable Reconciliation in Divided Societies.** Washington, D.C.:

U.S. Institute of Peace. Lederach, J.P. (2003) **The Little Book of Conflict Transformation.** Intercourse (PA): Good Books. McCready, S. (2001) **Empowering People.** Belfast: The Stationery Office.

Penn, William (first published 1693) **An Essay Towards the Present and Future Peace of Europe.** Brussels: republished by BOA Analysis Europe Ltd. in association with the Quaker Council for European Affairs (QCEA).

Pettigrew, John (1991) 'Quaker Mediation' in **Peacemaking in a**

Troubled World. Woodhouse, Tom (ed.) Oxford and Rhode Island: Berg Publishers.

Poole, David (2008) 'A Brief Overview of Quaker Relief and Peace-Making in Ireland' in Leahy, Brendan (ed.) **Interchurch Relations, Developments and Perspectives.** Dublin: Veritas 2008.

Punshon, John (1990) **Testimony and Tradition – Some Aspects of Quaker Spirituality.** Swathmore Lecture. London: Quaker Home Service.

QCEA Quaker Council for European Affairs (2007) **Women in Prison – A Review of Conditions in Member States of the Council of Europe.** Brussels: QCEA.

QCEA 1 2009 **The EU and the Western Balkans**.

QCEA 2 2009 **Mainstreaming Conflict Resolution**.

Quaker Faith and Practice (QFP) (1995) – The Book of Christian Discipline of the Yearly Meeting of the Religious Society of Friends (Quakers) in Britain: London: BYM

Ross, Marc Howard (2000) 'Creating the Conditions for Peacemaking: theories of practice in ethnic conflict resolution' **Ethnic and Racial Studies** Vol. 23 No. 6 Nov. 2000. Routledge Journals, Taylor and Francis Ltd.

Whitmire, Catherine (2007) **Practicing Peace.** Notre Dame (IN): Sorin Books.

Wigham, Maurice J. (1992) **The Irish Quakers.** Dublin: Historical Committee of the Religious Society of Friends in Ireland.

Woodham-Smith, Cecil (1991) **The Great Hunger – Ireland 1845-49.** London: Penguin.

Yarrow, C. H. Mike (1978) **Quaker Experiences in International Conciliation.** Newhaven and London: Yale University Press.

Chapter 2

SOME INITIATIVES OF FRIENDS

Arthur G Chapman

'Let your light shine' Matt.5.16 'It is better to light a candle than curse the darkness'
Chinese Proverb

This chapter describes the context in which local people were living during the Troubles and the contributions of groups of Quakers and individuals. It sets the scene, to some extent, for the larger initiatives described in Chapters 3-6.

INTRODUCTION

THE TROUBLES in Northern Ireland had repercussions on all citizens of the country and individual Friends were not exempt from their effects. Few members of Ulster Quarterly Meeting suffered the pressures felt by those who lived in housing estates controlled by paramilitaries or in isolated farms along the border, but meetings and individuals were disturbed by the general community unrest and challenged to express their faith in the light of these new developments. They responded in various ways both through the major schemes described in later chapters and in local or personal action.

Friends in Ulster number over 700 members in an area of the country largely settled by English planters in the 17th century, chiefly along the Lagan and Upper Bann valleys. Within the Quarterly Meeting there are two main traditions, one influenced by the evangelical movement of the 19th century with an emphasis on pietism and personal salvation and a strong Christian identity with other Protestant churches. It is strongly represented in meetings in the country west of Belfast. The other tradition is more concerned with social and political action and draws much from contemporary Quaker thought and practice in Britain. Its locus of influence is in the Greater Belfast area and the new meetings of Coleraine and Derry/Londonderry. A further dimension of Quaker action in Ulster is represented by the input of Friends from outside the Province, chiefly from Britain. Friends Service Council (now Quaker Peace and Social Witness), based in London, traditionally sought to bring healing to conflict situations in all parts of the globe and when violence arose within the jurisdiction of the UK itself, they felt bound to become involved in the resolution of these problems. Friends from outside Ulster became engaged on both a corporate and private level. (Chapman 1998)

Major Quaker projects tended to be located in the city of Belfast and thus from the beginning Friends in this area became most involved in the administration and implementation of initiatives such as the Service Committee (described in Chapter 3). Members across the Quarterly Meeting supported Quaker work, chiefly by providing volunteers for the prison canteens or by lending support when summer work camps took place in the neighbourhood. Many meetings were active in joint church initiatives to improve community relations. Country Friends were not so strictly segregated as those who live in the cities and major towns and they had a fair degree of natural interaction and cooperation with Catholic neighbours.

In the late 1960s there was a worldwide movement for Civil Rights and this found expression in Northern Ireland in a campaign for fairer representation of Catholics in local and parliamentary government and a removal of discrimination in employment and housing allocation. Many Friends had sympathy for these ideals but were disturbed when violence broke out in the wake of public demonstrations. Attacks on representatives of law and order provoked in turn a backlash from the Unionist community on demonstrators for Civil Rights. As a result their genuine grievances failed to be properly addressed and concessions by the establishment were only grudgingly granted. Sadly the issue of Civil Rights became lost as extremists on both sides inflamed passions which found expression in community strife and random indiscriminate destruction of life and property.

Friends were not immune from suffering and could identify with the many victims which the Troubles produced. One member of Grange Meeting was shot and fatally wounded as he returned home from work on his motorcycle; in Friends' School, Lisburn, a young female teacher lost a leg in an explosion outside a shop in Belfast and a Sixth Former was killed by a bomb which exploded prematurely as he travelled home by train. A Mission Hall near Lurgan, owned and run by local Friends, was destroyed by arson in 1974. Damage was also done to businesses owned by Friends through car bombs in various town centres.

People in business were frequently approached by strangers or anonymous groups seeking 'protection money' and offering to ensure that no harm came to the property. Such contributions were generally directed into the funds of paramilitary organisations. Those who declined to contribute showed much courage, knowing full well that a refusal could well mean retaliation by those who possessed the means and the will to destroy the business. One Friend in her office in Belfast was confronted once by a stranger who urgently demanded the keys of her car. She refused to hand them over, fearful that the car might be used for a wrongful purpose, and asked to know the reason for such a peremptory request. On hearing that it was to transport an injured man to hospital she consented to drive him there herself and showed considerable bravery in carrying out this mission.

The modus operandi of Quaker action is based on the concept of *concern*. By Divine impulse the individual is made aware of a particular need and shares this *concern* with other members of the group.* Thus action proceeds with the support of a wider base. It generally happens that the instigator also plays a major part in its implementation. The later chapters consider the major projects which involved Friends on a larger scale. The purpose of this chapter is to acknowledge the less dramatic, but nonetheless important, contribution of many Friends in Ulster Quarterly Meeting, as individuals, as meetings, or in joint action with other groups.

---

* See Christian Faith and Practice (London YM 1960) paras 363 and 364 for definition of Concern and also Chapter 1 section headed Testimonies and Concerns.

ULSTER QUAKER PEACE COMMITTEE

From the earliest times Friends have sought to promote peace and justice in society and the Ulster Quaker Peace Committee is of long standing as are the roots of conflict in Ireland. When conditions worsened in 1969 the Peace Committee became greatly involved in dealing with the practical outcomes of the conflict and the need to give immediate support to those who were suffering from it. In March 1970 the need was so great that it was decided to set up a special Service Committee (see Chapter 3) and allow the Peace Committee to concentrate on ideological issues concerning conflict both in Ireland and worldwide.

In these early years change was occurring at a bewildering rate and the Peace Committee was eager to involve all Friends in the Quarterly Meeting and be assured of their support. To that end frequent open meetings were held at centres outside Belfast, such as Bessbrook, Brookfield, Lurgan, Moyallon and Richhill. A booklet setting out the basis of the Quaker Peace Testimony was circulated widely in 1973. (UQPC 1973) A special Quarterly Meeting was convened at Brookfield in February 1975 to consult on the role of the Peace Committee and to consider public statements made in the name of Friends. The following minute was agreed:

'A full and heart-searching discussion has been followed through with the reconciling reminder that the Holy Spirit can work through all who earnestly endeavour to maintain the unity of the Spirit in the Bond of Peace. The Peace Committee's aim is to try to bring reconciliation between people with differing points of view and who may find it hard to recognise the Light of Christ in an opponent or to "live in that life and power which takes away the occasion of all wars". It has been stressed that the work of the Peace Committee is needed much at this time and that its role is both educative and informative, but if it wishes to bring statements and concerns before the public it should satisfy itself that the statement would have the general support of the Quarterly Meeting.'

(UQM Mins 1975)

In the early years of the Troubles there was much cooperation with established bodies such as the Fellowship of Reconciliation and Northern Friends Peace Board*. The worsening situation brought into being many other local groups, including the Peace People. This cooperation was fruitful and productive and many Friends were involved in vigils and public demonstrations. The arrival of concerned Quaker workers such as Will Warren in Derry and English and American Friends in Frederick Street Meeting House provided an opportunity for further action. Frequent requests were received from Britain and elsewhere to explain what was happening in Northern Ireland and to advise on how best to be helpful. Many members attended meetings in England and took part in consultations to ensure wise and informed involvement by outside bodies and individuals.

Another dimension in their work was 'speaking truth to power' (see Chapter 1). Government authorities were constantly lobbied on issues which Friends felt were detrimental to the resolution of the problems. Matters such as internment, riot control, the use of torture and plastic bullets, reintroduction of capital punishment were topics of correspondence with the Northern Ireland Office or other authorities. Advocacy was undertaken on behalf of victims or in cases where miscarriage of justice appeared to have taken place, such as with the Guildford Seven, the Armagh Four and the Birmingham Six. Involvement in the Peace Train Campaign is described in Chapter 5. One particular issue was condemnation of the use of toy guns and local traders were lobbied to have the sale of these products discontinued in their shops. However, the Peace Committee considers that their major contribution during the years of the Troubles was the Peace Education Project which they initiated and developed. It forms the content of Chapter 4 of this book.

IRISH YOUNG FRIENDS WORK CAMPS

Early in the Troubles Young Friends were concerned with the deteriorating situation in many segregated housing areas and with commendable alacrity and initiative made plans for a work camp in West Belfast. They advertised the project in the Irish Young Friends Quarterly for the spring of 1970. Here is an extract from

---

* Based in the North of England.

the letter written by two young Friends, Felicity McKerr and David Bass:

'Dear Friends,

Irish Young Friends Committee have decided to run a work-camp in Northern Ireland this year. This is being organised by a sub-committee called Irish Quaker Work Camps. We have found a play scheme project through the Voluntary Service Bureau in Belfast.

The project will take place in Ballymurphy, an overcrowded, 1950s housing estate in West Belfast, from Friday 17th July till Saturday 8th August. Volunteers will live in Ballymurphy Community Centre and provide play for some 200 children aged 10-12 in an area where there are no play facilities at present. In the next few months we will be working for the provision of playgrounds, so that we can leave something permanent after the workcamp. We are co-operating with Ballymurphy Tenants' Association and schools and churches in the area.'

(IYFQ 1970)

In the next issue of the IYF Quarterly a very frank report was given of the project which had demanded considerable enterprise and planning. A total of 18 international volunteers participated in the scheme, some recruited by Quaker Work Camps (QWC) London. They occupied around 200 children in games, craft and excursions for a period of three weeks. The report gives a flavour of the excitement of those times and the ways in which the abnormal circumstances impinged on the lives of children during summer holidays. With a breakdown of law and order and an atmosphere of revolt against authority it was no easy matter to provide a constructive programme. Problems were encountered with vandalism and the counter attraction of recreational rioting directed against the army. However, good contacts were made with the local tenants' association and an excursion to the seaside – a new and different environment – proved particularly successful.

Undeterred by the difficulties of 1970, Young Friends repeated the work camp at the same venue until 1974 during years when tension was again high. The presence of Felicity McKerr who was for part of this time a permanent youth worker in the estate and of four medium-term volunteers who spent the whole summer in

Ballymurphy enabled long term community involvement. More premises became available and a wider range of activities could be practised. Trips to the local hills and the swimming baths proved popular and excursions by bus were always a great success.

Tension in the area was particularly high in 1971 when the end of the work camp coincided with the introduction of internment. In a postscript to the leader's report David Bass wrote:

'Several work campers stayed on after the camp to help the medium term volunteers continue the playscheme in a more limited way. However, events made this turn out differently because by Monday morning (9th August) the situation had deteriorated so much that it was not possible to continue the scheme. However, the volunteers remaining proved of invaluable assistance in the troubles that followed by helping evacuate thousands of women and children, looking after them in various locations and providing first aid for those in need of it.... Unfortunately the trouble left its mark. On the Wednesday morning the Youth Leader, Paddy McCarthy died of a heart attack.' (QWC report 1971)

In 1973 and 1974 the number of outside volunteers was reduced to encourage more community participation, although there were frustrations because of the large numbers of women and children who chose to escape the difficulties of life on the estate by taking a holiday south of the border. There was involvement by a limited number of Irish Young Friends but the exercise was a bold and courageous one in that it reached out to a community with whom Friends in Ireland had very limited contact and earned for Quakers an acceptance which was of future value in their contacts in that area. As well as supporting these schemes, QWC in London arranged camps for children with learning disabilities in Ballycastle and Bushmills from 1970 till 1972 and another for children in the Protestant Shankill area, based on the Hammer Playground, in 1971 and 1972.

In subsequent years a variety of work camps were held both in Belfast and other towns by QWC and other organisations such as the Fellowship of Reconciliation, drawing on the experience gained by these original projects. During John and Diana Lampen's time in Derry the Quaker Youth Theatre came several summers for their Theatre-go-Round. The Lampens coordinated the visits and arranged for volunteers to work with children in both loyalist and nationalist housing estates and with British Army children.

BESSBROOK FRIENDS COMMUNITY RELATIONS ACTIVITY

This shows an example of what Friends in a local meeting did. Other meetings were also involved in cross-community activity.

Of all the historic Friends' meetings in the province of Ulster, Bessbrook is the only one which is situated in a predominately Catholic and republican area. This has shaped the response that Bessbrook Friends made to the conflict. Sometimes the reaction was fear and disgust and anger, other times there was moral and physical courage and some small efforts at making a witness with others towards peace and understanding.

In the late 1960s there was a work camp arranged from Britain at which Irish and overseas Young Friends toiled in the Derrymore House estate. In the evenings they made some contact with local young people. A few years later, in the 1970s there were several attempts to bomb and destroy Derrymore House, the National Trust property which was the home of the Baillie family. Edmund Baillie, clerk of Bessbrook Meeting, amazingly, carried a bomb away from the premises on at least two occasions, to protect his two sisters and brother. By 1976, attending Meeting entailed going through a military check-point close to the meeting-house avenue. During meeting, the silent communion was often shattered by helicopter activity from the nearby army base. Foot patrols, with blackened faces, would peer in through the windows, while the meeting dwelt on the words, 'None shall make them afraid'.

After the start of the Peace People in 1976, a Peace Group was set up in Newry, and a few Friends joined. In conjunction with the local Pax Christi there were occasional vigils held on the streets at times of high tension. Another, unpublicised, activity by the Newry Peace Group was visits to local families bereaved by the violent conflict. The visitors were always received courteously, whether the bereaved was a stunned mother of an IRA lad killed by his own bomb, or the desolate widow of a man shot while driving home from work at midday in Newry, as he had some association with army cadets.

By 1981 the local H-Block Support Committee approached the Peace Group looking for endorsement of their cause. A careful written response was given. This did not satisfy the republican activists who continued to lobby the group. Though there was no explicit intimidation, the Peace Group were all relieved when their visits stopped. The death of hunger-strikers inflamed the anger and resentment in the locality. When a hunger striker from near to Bessbrook died, one member of the meeting visited the bereaved family, but was not well received.

Another practical outlet for a few Friends in Bessbrook Meeting was in the cross-community Alliance Party. This brought opportunities to meet and discuss ideas for a shared future for all in Northern Ireland, along with an acceptance of Irish Unity if a majority voted for it. One member stood as an Alliance candidate in the local elections and courageously canvassed for votes in territory where partisan flags waved aggressively. She received little support and was not elected.

In 1995, Gerd and Christel Wieding, German Quakers, came for some days prior to the Friends Yearly Meeting in Dublin that year. They requested that they might meet privately with a range of political opinion in the local area. They met with a member of Bessbrook Meeting who was a policeman, with a family of devoted Catholics and with a Sinn Fein activist, Davy Hylands. During their time with him he asked them if it would be possible for them to visit Donna Maguire, a Newry woman held on remand in Germany on bombing charges. The Wiedings made at least one visit to her and, by their humane action, Bessbrook Quakers gained some credibility as Christian peacemakers with local Sinn Fein.

At some time in the late 1990s some Newry Protestants, realising that their numbers had halved in the previous 20 years, asked the local District Council for help to stem the exodus. The Council generously allocated funds and sponsored meetings to which a range of residents were invited along with some Councillors and Council staff. Brendan McAllister, a Newry man and Director of Mediation Northern Ireland was engaged as organiser. He proved to be a splendid chairman of the subsequent meetings. At first no Sinn Fein members were invited but it was soon realised that, despite Unionist misgivings, the meetings must be representative of all views within the town. The group became known as Newry Community Relations Forum. The proportion of Protestants attending the Forum was much greater than the 4% of the Newry population they made up. This was to acknowledge their sense of feeling beleaguered, unsafe and unwelcome in Newry and also because Orange and Black* marches were being restricted at this time. The Forum meetings were a new experience. Each one could express deep feelings without being shouted down or ridiculed. There was role-play to help us appreciate opposing views, then tea and buns together to share stories and listen to experiences. One memorable visit was to the Maze former prison site and the H-Blocks and hospital cells where hunger strikers died. Despite much emotive language, one could openly question the so-called heroism of those whose respect for human life was minimal, whether their own or their enemies. For some, the cause overruled every consideration.

One of the discoveries made was how secular the republican group had become. They openly declared that their attachment to the Catholic Church was finished. One of their group, Brian Campbell, died suddenly while out jogging. He was a gentle, articulate and persuasive member of the Forum who had earlier served a prison sentence for violence. He famously declared to his comrades on leaving jail, 'You can fight for Ireland, but I'm going to write for Ireland'. He became a journalist and speech writer for Sinn Fein politicians. There was no shred of religious words, no priest, no symbols at his funeral; but crowds of men in berets and uniform jackets and an address by a party leader.

The Protestant group in the Forum complained about Newry being bedecked by Tricolours and republican graffiti. One had to ask them to consider the plight of Catholics, say in Newtownards, smothered by Union Jacks. Can you do something to ease their predicament where the boot is on the other foot? The Forum continued until 2006 when, perhaps, its purposes had been largely fulfilled. Important insights were gained, less estrangement is now felt, so that the Forum did strengthen good relations among a diverse group who had a common interest in a better future for Newry.

In 2007, a Friends World Committee for Consultation (FWCC) international conference took place in Ireland. Prior to the conference about 20 of the delegates with a special inter-

---

* Refer to Glossary for Orange Order and Black Preceptory.

est in reconciliation came to Bessbrook Meeting House to learn about local steps towards peace. The Chief Executive of Newry and Mourne Council attended, along with several Forum members, and, with some satisfaction, told of the success of the Forum in fostering mutual understanding; a success in which there was some Quaker input.

NORTH-SOUTH CONTACT

Victor Bewley, a Dublin Friend, had contact with IRA leaders in the 1970s and 1980s, described in detail in his biography (Murdoch 2002). He had a concern that Republicans and members of the Northern unionist community could meet and hear each other's views about the future of Ireland, North and South. In cooperation with Friends and others in Ulster, he organised meetings in Bessbrook and South Belfast Meeting Houses, when people drawn from Quakers, the Orange Order, and various Unionist groupings were able to meet and exchange views with Republican sympathisers from Dublin. Some of these meetings are reported as having been 'hot and heavy', both groups stating their views in a forthright manner. There was little thought of compromise on either side at this stage and not always a clear understanding of the varying views on each side of the conflict. This was an early example of an attempt to encourage direct communication between opposing factions in the hope of increasing understanding. The meetings were private and were not reported at the time.

PUBLIC PRAYER MEETINGS IN PORTADOWN

During the 1980s and 90s one of the most intractable problems which affected community harmony was concerned with the issue of parades. This was looked upon as a traditional right by marchers regardless of its effect on the residents of the area through which they walked. The situation was exacerbated by population movement and new developments which meant that parades which were formerly on routes where they were welcomed or tolerated were now faced with a hostile reception.

In Portadown an Orange Order parade to Drumcree Church some two miles from the town centre on a Sunday morning in early July had been taking place annually for over 150 years. It passed through a Nationalist area on the outward trek and returned to town on a country road peopled chiefly by Protestants. In the 1980s protests caused the outward route to be changed but there was much controversy about the return journey. Because of redevelopment this area was inhabited mainly by Catholics and residents made it clear that the parade was not welcome. In 1995 the security forces refused permission for the Orange marchers to return along the Garvaghy Road after the Drumcree service. Eventually after several days they were allowed to return along this route to the town centre, escorted by security forces, but to the great annoyance of local residents. In the following years early July was a tense time in Portadown and throughout the entire Province. (Moloney 2007 p.466)

The local Friends Meeting was concerned at the situation and in 1996 arranged for the Meeting House to be open for prayer at lunchtime once a week during the month of June. The Meeting House is situated in the centre of the town and is readily accessible by all. It was made clear that Friends had no preconceived solution, but continued a regular monthly cross community prayer meeting in the Meeting House to seek the wisdom of God in the tense situation for those entrusted with making decisions and for those involved in the standoff. Portadown Meeting is a small group, but they were encouraged by the support of Friends throughout the Province, from churches in the town and some members of both groups associated with the confrontation. Some idea of the range of backgrounds represented can be gauged from the participation of the rector of Drumcree and at least one member of the Residents' Coalition committee from Garvaghy Road. This was a unique meeting place for people who would not come together in any other circumstances at that time.

Meetings were held once a month all year and more frequently in the month of June, until the parade in 1999, when the level of confrontation was greatly reduced and fears of total community strife had lessened. Friends acknowledged that prayers had been answered but continued in the Meeting House a regular monthly cross-community prayer meeting to intercede for the harmony and welfare of the town and country. It continues to the present day. The profile of Friends in the town was raised and links with the local churches greatly strengthened.

FRIENDS' INPUT INTO OTHER RECONCILIATION INITIATIVES

As the situation in Northern Ireland deteriorated during the early 1970s, so many groups became concerned with ways in which violence might be resolved and the underlying causes addressed. Friends gladly lent their support to many of these initiatives and sought thereby to have their voice heeded in government and to mould public opinion towards a more peaceful and just society.

Ireland Yearly Meeting is a founder member of the Irish Council of Churches which was set up in 1923 and Friends have always sought to influence this body as to the need to promote peace and reconciliation among communities on the island. However, the Irish Council of Churches did not include in its membership the Roman Catholic Church and thus its authority was somewhat limited. During the unrest at the beginning of the 1970s many were aware of this deficiency and discussions were held on ways to promote harmony and cooperation and reduce violence in the country. A special meeting was convened at Ballymascanlon, near Dundalk, in 1973 with equal numbers of Catholic and non-Catholic members to consider matters of faith and address the current social unrest. (Hurley & Ellis 1998) A series of meetings in subsequent years received reports on social issues from joint working parties on which Friends were prominently represented. For example, in 1976 a report was submitted on 'Violence in Ireland' from a panel which included the Belfast Friend, Denis Barritt. (Daly & Gallagher 1976) In 1990 a hard-hitting report on Northern Ireland's Prisons came from a group which included John Lampen, at that time resident in Derry. (IICM1990) He was also the co-Chair with Mary McAleese, now President of Ireland, of a group which produced a discussion document on Sectarianism. (IICM 1993) Since 1970 David Poole, of Dublin, has been on the Executive Council, being Chairman of ICC and co-Chair of the Ballymascanlon Conference in 1984 and 1985. At a local level many Friends were active on Councils of Churches in their own towns and neighbourhoods, bearing witness to peace and fostering practical ways of reducing tension. (Poole, D. 2008)

On the political front many Friends were disturbed by the sharp divide between Unionist and Nationalist parties which meant that the constitutional issue was ever to the fore to the neglect of matters of social and economic concern. The New Ireland Movement was founded in 1969 with Friend Brian Walker as Chairman. It sought to mobilize moderate public opinion to counteract the increasing political extremism and from this movement emerged the Alliance Party. A number of Friends were active in this political party and at least one member served as a local Councillor. During the years of the Troubles many efforts were made to advise on the way forward from the political stalemate in which the country was placed and Friends served on such bodies as the Cadogan Group and the Faith and Politics Group, seeking to develop a peace process for the country. One Friend was on the steering committee of the Evangelical Contribution on Northern Ireland (ECONI). Through conferences, courses and seminars ECONI* sought to challenge mainly the Protestant constituency to apply the essential message of the Gospel to the contemporary situation.

Because of the traditional segregation of Ulster society contacts across the religious divide were limited. To counteract this tendency Protestant and Catholic Encounter (PACE) was set up in 1969. Denis Barritt, who was active and vocal in many peace and reconciliation movements, became the founding co-Chair of what was essentially a lay movement. Its value was in providing a forum where Protestants and Catholics could meet on an equal basis, visit each other's churches and discuss essential matters of their faith and practice. (Barritt, D. 1982 Ch.6)

The violence and atrocities of major incidents in the Troubles always called forth strong condemnation but this expression was often of an emotional nature which concentrated on laying blame on 'the other side'. Friends welcomed expressions of revulsion at violence but longed for a deeper search for genuine commitment to reconciliation. This appeared to come in the popular movement of the Peace People, led by women in West Belfast. Their rallies in both Catholic and Protestant areas attracted much support and earned for the leaders the Nobel Peace Prize in 1977. Friends were happy to encourage this grassroots movement and were pleased that a Friend, Peter McLachlan, gave wise leadership to the movement, becoming its Chairman in 1978.

In Derry the Peace People movement became the Peace and Reconciliation Group (PRG) and developed in its own way. Initially it was inspired by the work of Will Warren, an English Friend

* Now The Centre for Contemporary Christianity.

29

who had come to Derry with a Fellowship of Reconciliation work camp in 1971 and remained in the city, building up a network of contacts from church leaders to loyalist and republican paramilitaries. (Harrison 2008 W. Warren) The trust he had built up was inherited and enhanced by work carried on by John and Diana Lampen, also English Quakers, who after their arrival in the early 1980s became active in the PRG. As well as carrying out conventional community work, the PRG did much to improve relations between the nationalist community and the RUC and at a later stage by slow and patient negotiation managed to reduce the level of violence in the city between the Army and the IRA. In fact it has been suggested that the Derry experiment in de-escalation of violence was a precursor of the general IRA ceasefire of 1994.

It is virtually impossible to record all the actions of both Ulster and visiting Friends to bring about understanding and reconciliation, often in small ways, during the conflict. Some were public and spectacular, others were personal and discreet. Following the Light of Christ, Will Warren by his simple honesty and fearless, persistent efforts to show his loving concern gained the trust of major participants in the Derry conflict. The Lisburn Friend, Arnold Benington, a noted naturalist, was invited by the BBC to present a Schools Programme on 'Nature in the Inner City'. Through this project he developed a real friendship with the staff and pupils of St. Mary's Primary School in the Lower Falls. He was invited to take school assembly and also arranged football matches with teams from his own town.

For most ordinary Friends life had to continue its normal pattern, but they showed courage and enterprise in how they went about their daily routine. It meant for those in business resisting intimidation and guaranteeing fair employment practice; for farmers working together, especially at harvest time, with neighbours of a different political and religious persuasion; for teachers in making schools places of security and stability for children whose home life was disturbed by all sorts of intolerable pressures. By professing allegiance to a higher power than political or community pressure or paramilitary authority, by refusing to take sides, by speaking out against prejudice and injustice, by seeking meaningful contacts across the political divide, Friends in Ulster bore witness to the reality of their faith.

References

Barritt, D. (1982), **Northern Ireland. A Problem to Every Solution,** Ch.6, London: Quaker Peace & Service and Northern Friends Peace Board.

Chapman, A. (1998), 'The Religious Society of Friends (Quakers)' in Richardson, N. (ed.), **A Tapestry of Beliefs: Christian Tradition in Northern Ireland,** Belfast: Blackstaff Press.

Daly, C. and Gallagher, E. (1976), **Violence in Ireland,** Report to the Churches.

Harrison, Richard S. (2008) **A Biography of Irish Quakers II,** Dublin: Four Courts Press.

Hurley, Rev. M. and Ellis, Dr. I. (1998), **Irish Inter-Church Meeting – Background and Development:** Irish Inter-Church Meeting (IICM).

Ireland Yearly Meeting (2008), **Minutes and Appendices,** Quaker House, Dublin.

Irish Inter Church Meeting (IICM) Dept of Social Issues (1990), **Northern Ireland's Prisons:** IICM.

Irish Inter Church Meeting (IICM) Dept of Social Issues (1993), **Sectarianism:** IICM.

Irish Young Friends Quarterly (1970), **Spring and Autumn issues.**

Memories of participants in Work Camps, in conversation with author.

Moloney, E. (2007), **A Secret History of the IRA,** p.466, London: Penguin Books.

Poole, D. (2008), 'A Brief Overview of Quaker Relief and Peace-Making in Ireland' in Leahy, B. (ed.), **Inter-church Relations Developments and Perspectives,** Dublin: Veritas.

Portadown Preparative Meeting (1993), **Reports and Minutes.**

Quaker Work Camps (1971), **Reports of Work Camps Committee,** London.

Ulster Quaker Peace Committee (1960-2000), **Minutes and Reports.**

Ulster Quaker Peace Committee (1973), **Quaker Peace Testimony booklet.**

Ulster Quarterly Meeting (1975), **Minutes of Meetings.**

Voluntary Service Bureau, Belfast (1970-5), **Correspondence and Reports.**

Chapter 3

ULSTER QUAKER SERVICE

Roy Blair

'…In as much as you have done it to one of the least of my brethren, you did it to me….'
Matt.25.40

INTRODUCTION

THIS CHAPTER describes the development of a Quaker service organisation which emerged as a response to the outbreak of sectarian violence in 1969. It traces the growth of the charity from its beginning by a concerned group of Quaker volunteers anxious to respond to immediate and urgent need. Over the last 40 years Quaker Service has emerged as a professional family and childcare agency providing a range of support and therapeutic services in the largest prison in Northern Ireland and at a cross community family centre in West Belfast.

Quakers have, for the 350 years of their history sought to live out their Christian beliefs. In Ireland, although relatively small in numbers, Friends have supported the vulnerable irrespective of religion, race or creed. They were ready to respond where issues of social justice needed a voice. When the riots in Belfast erupted in 1969 there quickly followed looting, burning of houses, and families fleeing the danger and destruction. A small group of Friends came together determined to reach out to people in need. Within a few months they formed the Belfast Friends Emergency Committee, with the support of Quaker Meetings throughout

Ulster. From those small beginnings there has emerged a vibrant and dynamic charity. This is not just the story of a committee of Friends but of a community, bitterly divided, needing a caring and healing influence. Friends were led by the Spirit of God to reach out to the most vulnerable in a society torn apart by fear and bitterness.

That August many families needed immediate refuge from the carnage. While the men remained to protect the houses women and children were cared for in church halls. Frederick Street meeting house was at this time an old traditional Quaker building and for several days families used it as a night shelter to protect them from street violence. Friends supplied pillows and blankets and tea and sandwiches were made each day. After some days the level of violence subsided and the families made alternative arrangements. However it was evident that no one was sure of the future and Friends had a sense that their response could be needed for some time.

ESTABLISHING A COMMITTEE

The first recorded meeting of the Belfast Friends Emergency Committee took place in September 1969 in the home of a Friend with 6 Quakers present. By the third meeting which was held 3 weeks later in South Belfast Meeting House, the number had grown to 17 drawn from a number of local meetings, with 3 apologising for absence. At this meeting the group, influenced by the extent of continued violence and disruption, agreed to give whatever help they could. The minute of the meeting reads:

'We have discussed possible openings for service and reconciliation both now and in the future. These include:

(a) Use of Meeting Houses as meeting places for Catholics and Protestants.

(b) Help with existing playgroups including those run by SCF (Save the Children Fund) and NSPCC (National Society for the Prevention of Cruelty to Children).

(c) Collecting names of Friends willing to work as volunteers.

34

(d) Giving financial help to the Belfast Housing Aid Society which provides deposits on houses for private purchase.'

Belfast Friends Emergency Committee Mins 1969

Ulster Quarterly Meeting (UQM) at its 27th September 1969 meeting endorsed the establishment of the group and its proposed actions. The Emergency Committee became a sub committee of UQM Peace and Service Committee. (UQM Mins 1969)

Over the next few months individual Friends within the Committee pursued a variety of activities. Some concentrated on playgroups and holiday schemes, others focused on work parties where they engaged in activities in various housing estates and some helped with reconciliation initiatives. Whilst most of the work was undertaken by local Friends, the first full-time volunteer from Britain, David Le Mare, arrived in February 1970 to support and develop schemes under the aegis of the Committee. It was apparent at this time that the Committee, deeply concerned about the ongoing strife and violence, was searching for a function and role in relation to people affected by the conflict, locally known as the Troubles. Northern Ireland was in turmoil, socially as well as politically, and it was often a case of responding to an immediate need rather than any planned development or response.

INTERNMENT, RESPONSES AND THE FORMATION OF UQSC

On 11th August 1971 internment without trial was introduced by the British Government and hundreds of men from the Catholic community were forcibly removed to a former British Army Camp at Long Kesh. This was some three miles from the nearest town, Lisburn. In the immediate aftermath there was further violence and upheaval across Belfast and other towns. The Committee focused on the impact of potential large scale movement of families and the need for emergency centres. By this stage there was cooperation and coordination with the local Welfare Department in Belfast and more practical help was available to families.

By October 1971 it was evident that the Committee needed help with the organisation and administration of its now diverse work. The decision was taken to appoint an Organising Secretary on a part-time basis. Margaret McNeill, a Friend with experience

35

of Relief work after the Second World War agreed to take the post from November with an office based in South Belfast meeting house. At the meeting of the Peace and Service Committee in November 1971 two significant features of the life of the Committee were recorded. The first was an agreement to explore how to help the relatives of the men in Long Kesh during visiting time. Secondly, the first formal planning meeting was arranged, something which was to become a key feature in the future. Among the proposals for development from that meeting were:

- *'The provision of a Quaker minibus*
- *Holiday centre for families (caravan accommodation)*
- *Rest room for relatives visiting Long Kesh Camp*
- *Outings for children*
- *Visiting of old or lonely people*
- *Families to be accommodated at Corrymeela'.*
  (a residential centre at Ballycastle)

These suggestions were to play a prominent part in the development of this small organisation over the next two decades. A further proposal which was passed to the Peace Committee was the possibility of a Quaker House in Belfast (see Chapter 5).

In December 1971 a submission was made to the Ministry of Home Affairs to provide facilities so that refreshments could be served to visitors at Long Kesh. Friends were invited by Government to organise and manage these arrangements. But crucially prisoners' relatives from West Belfast also met the Committee and requested them to provide a service at the prison, so the request came from both parties involved. The service was made available from mid January 1972 and consisted of a canteen provision, staffed by a volunteer rota on five days per week. This was the first Prison Visitors' Centre in Northern Ireland and among the first in the UK. It was the forerunner of the Prison work described later in this chapter. At the same time a minibus was acquired and began providing transport to a number of voluntary groups caring for vulnerable and disabled people, mainly in the Belfast area. Work continued on holiday schemes and work camps as part of a number of short term initiatives (see Chapter 2).

In March 1972 there was a discussion in the Peace and Service committee about the difference in emphasis between peace work and service work and the need to clarify responsibilities. Ulster

36

Quarterly Meeting (UQM) agreed to change the name to Ulster Quaker Service Committee (UQSC) and this was to be the name under which a range of services developed during the next 36 years. The already existing UQ Peace Committee followed another path (see Chapter 6). In July of 1972 the new Committee saw the possibility of a continuing need for a Visitors' Centre post internment. It was agreed to take up discussion with the Ministry. The minute records: *'should internment end completely before our next meeting we shall suspend this service'!* Although internment was gradually phased out the camp was redesignated as HMP Maze Prison and the service not only stayed, but grew to provide a range of support services for visitors and prisoners. Monica Barritt of South Belfast Meeting joined the Committee in January 1973 and in March of that year was offered the post of the Maze Canteen Organiser. Monica set about organising the canteen and developing regular contact with the prison authorities.

A VISION FOR THE FUTURE

At this stage Friends were alive to the need not only to provide immediate help to families and communities affected by the Troubles but in two other key areas for the future of Ulster, namely, criminal justice and reconciliation. The development of a Visitors' Centre at the Maze Prison brought UQSC firmly into the first of these fields. In regard to the second, although the Committee did not see itself involved directly in reconciliation work, a key principle of its function was to reconcile individuals and communities, where possible. They identified an opportunity to encourage Ulster Friends to have a specific role in reconciliation with the opening of the new Quaker Meeting House in Frederick Street in 1973. A caretaker's flat was attached to the meeting house and the Committee promoted the concept that this might be used by the Friends in Residence to work quietly for peace and reconciliation within and between communities. One of the reasons for considering this possibility was the regard for Quakers in both Catholic and Protestant communities. There was a sense of being neither one nor the other but occupying some kind of middle ground with trust and respect from both sides of the community. This work was later to be taken up by Quaker House (see Chapter 5). Later, a staff member was to record the following anecdote:

'and the thing that was great for me, and made my job easier was that you just went to these areas and said you were from the Quakers and it was no problem. They just assumed I was a Quaker, I never said it, but they assumed it, and I ... was brought up a Catholic.... But soon as you rapped the door and said I am from the Quakers they would say', ahh the Quakers, they are good people'. It gave a great opening and people didn't see it as a threat'.

Bischoff, C.D. 2006

The work continued to grow during the remainder of the decade, often interrupted by outbreaks of violence, political unrest, major bombings and shootings with serious loss of life. The Committee continued to provide the canteen facilities at the Maze. The building and part of the prison were burnt down in 1974 in a prison riot. The canteen moved into a new purpose built building in 1975 with improved facilities, providing some hot inexpensive food, a place to rest, toilets etc., which were appreciated by many families. For many reasons wives or partners brought their children to the prison. When they arrived often after a lengthy journey there could be a considerable wait at the Visitors' Centre. It did not take long for the Committee to realize that something needed to be provided for the children. Early in 1975 Save the Children Fund agreed to organise the first playgroup at the new Visitors' Centre. A room was set aside and stocked with appropriate play materials. Mothers could relax, knowing that their children could play nearby in a safe and secure environment. No one anticipated the extent to which these services would become a core feature of Quaker work at the Centre and eventually inside the prison itself.

In the South Belfast area a lunch club and holiday scheme for older people commenced. The number of work camps increased providing opportunities for young people from other countries to join with local groups to organise some facilities for children and make general improvements in the area (see Chapter 2 Workcamps section). Every opportunity was taken to provide holiday schemes for families and children and the minibus service was stretched to its limit to service some 50 voluntary organisations each year. These practical services were a valuable resource to a number of communities as Belfast, in particular, had become a series of segregated areas with little movement outside of them. The focus of the work was in the areas directly affected by violence and sectarian tension. They were mainly in the Catholic and Protestant areas of West and North Belfast which experienced some of the worst of the Troubles.

REVIEW, STAFFING AND NEW DIRECTIONS

In January 1979 the Committee carried out a further review of its work since its inception. The minutes of the monthly meeting of UQSC reflect the extent of its activities over the previous few years. These included supporting volunteer workers in the community, a minibus service, the Maze Prison canteen incorporating a playgroup and advice centre, holidays for children, families and senior citizens and a lunch club. The minutes record the continued enthusiasm to develop further the lunch clubs, to expand the minibus service and provide an after hours centre for school children.

The Committee continued discussions on future projects during the year, when an invitation came from the Craigavon Council for Refugees to support a Vietnamese family coming to live in Craigavon. At this time many Vietnamese families were fleeing their country with the takeover of the new communist government. They were known round the world as the 'boat people'. The UK Government accepted a quota of the refugees and councils agreed to provide homes and support with education and employment. Craigavon Council welcomed a number of families and different churches offered to host individual families to help them settle in their new community. The Committee agreed to raise funds to support the family and looked to local Friends to provide help and assistance.

At this time, 1979, the staff consisted of the Organising Secretary, the Maze Canteen Organiser, an Assistant Organiser and a typist. When Margaret McNeill indicated that she was not able to give sufficient time to her post, it was agreed that the time was now right to place the work of the Organizing Secretary on a full-time basis with an enhanced job description and renamed Projects Organiser. Vincent Bent was appointed as the first full time Projects Organiser in March 1980. Anne Grant of South Belfast Meeting had been one of the early committee members and she agreed to take over the new part-time secretary's post. At the same time Joyce Neill, of South Belfast, who had been

Chair of UQSC since 1973 decided to stand down. Joyce had steered the work with wisdom and enthusiasm in the early years and during some very troubled times in Northern Ireland. Betty McElnea, a Friend from Frederick Street Meeting, agreed to take over the Chair. It was evident that Ulster Friends were committed to respond and prepared to step forward and take on considerable responsibilities as the work developed.

Work was started on some of the project ideas from the Committee. Encouraged by the success of the elderly persons' lunch club which met monthly in South Belfast meeting house, the Committee became aware of the needs of elderly confused persons, often very vulnerable and living alone. In late 1980 with a number of volunteers, Vincent established a weekly lunch club for a small number of people from the area close to the Meeting House. This scheme ran successfully until April 1985 when the statutory authorities had identified a need and provided a day hospital service at Belfast City Hospital. A number of members of the 'Wednesday Club' transferred to the new hospital service. Friends were pleased that the need for a service was recognised and that elderly confused people would receive a professional service designed to meet their needs. The Annual Report for that year records:

> 'The project had run for four and a half years, had been the first vol untary project of this kind in Northern Ireland and had contributed, we believe, to the recognition of the needs of a growing sector within our society. We are happy to have been involved in this work, and equally happy to let the statutory body take over and develop it'.
>
> *UQSC Annual Report 1985*

The monthly lunch club for elderly people continued until the early 1990s when it was decided to close. Falling numbers together with improved local statutory provision and support were the main factors, but again the Committee felt they had filled a gap at a difficult and turbulent time.

Meantime, the caravan scheme at Newcastle, Co.Down proved highly successful in providing a number of families, mainly from West Belfast, with a week's respite by the sea. A number of caravans were rented each year for a 4 week period. One caravan was used for volunteers who cared for and provided organised play for the children each day. This gave some 16 mothers the opportunity to relax. For most of these families this was the first time they experienced a holiday and travelling outside their area of Belfast. The caravan holiday scheme ran from 1980 to 1997. A review by the Committee in 1998 indicated that it would no longer be able to use the site at Newcastle. Other options were explored but none were found acceptable. It was with some regret that this scheme closed after 17 years.

A further project was proposed by Vincent. This was to work with a group of unemployed youths from the Lower Falls area. At this time unemployment in Northern Ireland stood at 14% but in deprived areas it could reach 50–75% of young males. His idea was to help them develop basic work skills in the renovation and maintenance of buildings and that this would assist them in seeking employment. With Government support the Committee employed a worker to assist Vincent and the scheme operated 5 days each week. The scheme continued until 1984 when it was decided to close. There was continuing difficulty in recruiting and retaining the trainees. Also the Government indicated that they intended to withdraw the funding and focus the work on a smaller number of large training centres which would provide the opportunity to experience a greater range of skills training.

In September 1980 Vincent brought a proposal to the Committee involving the use of a small holding on the slopes of Black Mountain in West Belfast. It consisted of an old single storey cottage with outbuildings and some rough pasture. The cottage was sited on the hill above and between some of the most deprived communities, Protestant and Catholic, with access lanes coming from each area. It had been uninhabited for five years and was in a very poor condition. However it was in an ideal position to offer a service to both communities and was available at a peppercorn rent for ten years. Nevertheless it took some vision and a considerable step of faith to go with the proposal to develop the site initially for children and young people on a cross-community basis. Quaker Cottage was born!

AN EMERGING STRATEGY

It may not have been apparent at the time, but this was a critical juncture in the life of UQSC. There were now two major features to its function as a voluntary agency: the prison work and the work based at the Cottage involving children but eventually to include mothers. There were other strands of the work; some lasted a number of years while others were short term. They were important for the contribution they made to the lives of individuals and families: the minibus service, support for the Vietnamese family, caravan holidays, lunch club and senior citizens holidays, to name but a few. All of these made a positive impact but it was right to close or transfer work that was either no longer required or better carried out by others. As the Prison and the Cottage became more complex, the emphasis shifted gradually from volunteers to paid staff. The other strand that continued from these early days was the concern to influence and promote changes and improvements in prison welfare policy and practices, based on the experiences from many families affected by them. These three strands, the prison work, Quaker Cottage and criminal justice policy and practice emerged as the main elements of a strategy for service provision by the Committee until the present time and are described in the following paragraphs.

1. WORK IN THE PRISONS

Quakers have a history of responding to prison issues. It's not a popular concern, perhaps due to a general public apathy towards prisoners and their families and also to government policy, with a focus largely on punishment rather than rehabilitation and restitution. Throughout its history the Religious Society of Friends has contributed to improvements within prisons and to the welfare of families and prisoners.

As the Long Kesh Camp became established as a prison, the British Government invited Quakers to provide facilities for visiting families. In those early years it was mainly a canteen facility while visitors waited to be transferred into the prison for a visit. However it began to provide much more than that. It is difficult to describe how distressing and emotional it can be for families to go through the process of a visit, often after a long journey on inadequate public transport perhaps with small children. The information, guidance and listening ear provided helped many to cope with the stress. Even after internment ended in 1978 and future prisoners were convicted, these services became an essential part of the Quaker Visitors' Centres. For various reasons families visiting the prison were at times not treated well. Visits were cancelled without warning or explanation. Often this was due to unrest or difficulties within the prison. Gradually Monica Barritt as Visitors' Centre Organiser was able to gain access to the authorities and to speak on the behalf of many distressed families. Greater opportunity was given to Quakers by the prison authorities to speak about the need for improvements, better services for visitors and their access to prisoners.

By 1982 the Visitors' Centre at the Maze was opened 6 days per week. The Committee began to experience difficulty in maintaining the number of volunteers to staff the canteen each day. The decision was taken to recruit some part-time staff to work alongside the volunteers. The playgroup organised by SCF was in place and working well and an Advice and Information Centre was available at the canteen. In 1983 a new Assistant Organiser Martie Rafferty, a Friend, was appointed and she succeeded Monica Barritt as Organiser on her retirement the following year. Martie, encouraged and supported by the Committee, sought to develop new directions from the solid foundation left by her predecessor.

Perhaps due to the trust Quakers had built with the Prison authorities, they allowed Martie greater internal access to prisoners and prison staff. The Maze, at this time, held mostly people who regarded themselves as political prisoners and not criminals. Tensions ran high on a regular basis. The 'blanket' protest and the hunger strike in 1981/82 created a complete breakdown in relationships and internal contact within the prison. Throughout the 1980s these protests became a focal point for conflict and spilt over into widespread violence in the community. As the Visitors' Centre Organiser, Martie had the opportunity to develop contact with prisoners and developed a network of contacts and relationships with republicans and loyalists, some of whom were key leaders in their organizations. In her visits they would often approach her with issues or concerns they felt were not being addressed. Martie had direct access to a number of prison governors and was able to raise matters quickly and perhaps help to ameliorate some potentially violent reactions during these turbulent years.

The first pre-release groups were established by Martie in 1985 because there was so little preparation in place for the release of prisoners. These provided an opportunity for wives and partners to prepare over a number of sessions for the homecoming. Later meetings of pre-release prisoners were organised to help them understand the effect of their release on relationships at home. The committee explored with the authorities the need to integrate this work with a support and follow up service in the community, seen to be a critical element in pre-release schemes. As no funding was available by the early 1990s, it was agreed that the pre-release and after care projects would be transferred to the Northern Ireland Probation Service.

A New Prison – Maghaberry

Given the growing size of the prison population in the 1980s, a new prison was planned at Maghaberry, again in the country some miles from the nearest towns of Moira and Lisburn. Such was the confidence in the Quaker work at the Maze, the Government invited the Committee to take responsibility for what became a modern purpose-built Visitors' Centre, opening in 1987. By this time the Committee had taken over responsibility for the playgroups at both the Maze and Maghaberry. Pre-release groups were started at the new prison and these involved, for the first time, women prisoners who had been transferred to Maghaberry from Armagh Jail when it closed.

Staffing arrangements changed during these years. With the requirement to maintain a service at both prisons, volunteers were gradually replaced by a number of paid part-time staff. The children's work required qualified workers to meet the stringent requirements of playgroup legislation. Recruiting and training staff became an important element in providing the level of emotional support often needed by visitors.

Recognition of the Work

The work of Quakers in the two prisons was recognised nationally in 1989 when the Committee was awarded the Butler Trust Award from its patron H.R.H the Princess Royal in London. It was a very proud moment for the volunteers and staff who had worked through such difficult times to build a place of care and support for many people affected by the Troubles.

In 1991 the Committee was again at the forefront of innovation in prison work. Maghaberry became the first in the UK to create childcare facilities within the prison. This allowed the fathers to re-engage with the children and enabled the children to enjoy constructive play with childcare staff near their parents. The childcare facility within the prison was re-sited and enlarged to provide better facilities for visiting families including a tea bar and a large open plan play area. Over the years there has been the most positive response by families to the provision of these services. The Committee has often received tributes to the care and support given by staff. Many are about the atmosphere and the warmth of the greeting or the cup of tea and sometimes the support given in a stressful situation. One mother recorded her reactions:

'There came a bad time at my husband's review when he got sent back for a few more years. To me it was the start of his sentence all over again. When I got the news on our visit, I was close to ending my life. The only thing I had going through my head was to get out to the Visitors' Centre. When I did get out and told them the news, they hurt as much as I did, but they gave me their support in every way'.

UQSC Annual Report 1993

The Good Friday Agreement and Beyond

The release of a large number of prisoners following the Good Friday Agreement in 1998 had immediate implications for the future of the Maze Prison which finally closed in 2000. It had always been regarded as a temporary prison. The Committee and the Projects Organiser dealt with the stress of closure for a number of staff who had worked so faithfully over a number of difficult years.

On her retirement from the staff, Monica Barritt returned to membership of the Committee and was Chairman from 1988 until 1992. She maintained her membership of the Committee until her untimely death in the summer of 1999. Monica left an indelible footprint on the development of UQSC and particularly in prison Visitors' Centre work. The Committee, determined to remember her commitment and dedication, secured an agreement from the prison authorities to name the Maghaberry Centre as the Monica Barritt Visitors' Centre. A Meeting for Worship with her sons and their families was held in the Centre in September 2000.

The present day make-up of the prison population is very different from the original inmates. The women's prison was re-sited to Hydebank Wood near Belfast and Maghaberry now houses both sentenced and remand adult male prisoners with a residue of 'political' prisoners. There were 829 in total at March 2008. Remand prisoners are allowed more frequent access to families and this has increased the activity within the Visitors' Centre considerably. It operates 6 days per week and continues to provide childcare facilities while families are waiting, a minibus to service the half mile to the prison gates, and a tea bar and childcare facilities and staff within the prison. In 2007/08 the activity level was recorded as:

Purchases at the Centre/Teabar 76,367
Attendance by children 16,110
Average number of children daily 54
Use of shuttlebus 48,357

These figures include use by families on a number of occasions during the year but they do give an indication of the extensive use made of the facilities.

The prison population is not only growing but is changing in the composition and ethnicity of the male population. Since the late 1990s Northern Ireland has seen a significant growth in ethnic minority groups from Europe and further afield. Regrettably there has been a consequent increase in the numbers of prisoners from these backgrounds. The Committee has responded in two ways. Initially its existing Guidance Booklet for visitors was translated into a number of languages. Secondly, as part of a new volunteer project in 2006 isolated prisoners were identified and contact offered. This included both foreign nationals and local prisoners. It is estimated that 10-15% of the prison population rarely or never receive a visit from anyone. A number of other schemes are being explored based on the use of trained volunteers. It is hoped that as resources become available new services will be added to meet the needs of an increasing prison population from diverse backgrounds. Friends are committed to providing the core services for families. These new initiatives demonstrate their openness to respond to new needs, and to build on the positive and constructive relationship with the prison authorities.

2. QUAKER COTTAGE

As mentioned earlier, the Cottage required some repairs before it could be used. Some of this was carried out by the young unemployed group and by a series of Quaker workcamps. By late 1980 the first of many full-time volunteers came to live there albeit in the most primitive of conditions. Initially they came from Britain, but gradually also from North America and Europe and this still continues. Some were Quakers, others were from a range of church or peace organizations. They became a crucial part of the love and care given to all who visited Quaker Cottage, a unique feature of the work at this site.

The volunteers began work with 5-11 year old children, starting with after school activities in drama, crafts and play. Some of these children came from families directly affected by the violence, perhaps a father or sibling killed or badly injured, sometimes as a result of a punishment shooting. All the children come from local communities imprisoned by fear, anxiety, sectarianism and prejudice. None of the children could escape the influence and attitudes of their communities.

By 1981 the Cottage was in a sufficient state of repair to allow a second volunteer to join the project. They commenced a range of activities with groups of children referred from the local areas. A prefabricated building was added in 1982 to provide basic residential accommodation for a number of volunteers who came for periods of 1-2 years. In these early years the focus of the work was to provide children, mainly in the 5-ll age group, with creative play opportunities. These were a daily after school group during the winter months increasing in the summer holidays to a day long play scheme.

A Family Centre

The Committee and Vincent, the Projects Organiser, gained valuable experience in this work with children. One of the full-time volunteers undertook some research and recommended to the Committee that encouragement should be given to mothers to share in and play with their children at the Cottage. From this emerged the concept of a family centre providing support and guidance to groups of mothers each week and a crèche/playgroup to care for children under 5. It was agreed that an important element of the programme was that the groups should be organised on a cross-community basis. Staff developed a relationship with the local Health & Social Services authority for two critical reasons. One, to secure some funding towards the new family service and secondly to ensure that they received appropriate referrals of mothers and their children who could benefit most. By October 1986 the first two groups of mothers commenced attendance at the Cottage.

By the following year it was becoming evident that the Cottage and its *modus operandi* had much to offer in supporting families under stress. The feedback from the mothers and from the statutory authorities was very positive about the benefits gained for the families. The buildings which were old or of a temporary nature were beginning to show signs of wear. The Committee agreed the need to plan for a complete replacement and modernisation of the site. The cost would be well in excess of £200,000 and would include a new residential house for the long-term volunteers. This was an enormous challenge, and again a big step of faith to find this level of funding and to commit to a long term project. The 1990 Annual Report gives a fascinating insight into the development of the work at the Cottage:

> *'What have we achieved in ten years? We certainly have not solved the problems, nor stopped the violence, but then we never expected to. We have, however, seen people change, 'new' women walking tall, laughing, challenging old ideas, and challenging systems which seem at times to have forgotten that they are there to serve people and not vice-versa. We have seen children beginning to trust, learning to co-operate, trying to understand nonviolence and certainly enjoying themselves. We are fortunate to have shared in people's joy and pain, to have listened and encouraged, to have cried and laughed along with them. They serve to keep us humble and remind us of the long, slow metamorphosis which has to take place ... before a lasting peace with justice will prevail'.*
> *UQSC Annual Report 1990*

These were almost prophetic words which have been the cornerstone of the work at Quaker Cottage right to this present time. Such was the respect for Friends' work in response to the Troubles that there was a groundswell of support for the building project.

Statutory authorities together with a grant from a Quaker trust secured the full amount and allowed the rebuilding to begin. During construction work, temporary premises were secured with support from the local housing authority, both for the groups and for the volunteers. The new buildings were opened in 1991 at a ceremony involving a Protestant and a Catholic mother representing the users of the Cottage in the past. Playgroup facility for the under 5s, meeting rooms for mothers, activity rooms for older children and outside play areas were all provided.

The work with mothers evolved over a period of time. It has, at its core, the Quaker belief in the intrinsic value and worth of each individual. The support is based on acceptance and love, giving each person the space and scope for reflection. Quakers hold, as a core element of their faith the need to be actively 'seeking that of God in everyone'. Staff at Quaker Cottage have incorporated this ethic into the culture and work with mothers and children, an approach recognised and valued not just by the Committee and staff but by the statutory authorities and users.

The programme is not highly structured but focuses on the needs of each group as they emerge in conversation and discussion. Each group consists of 7-9 mothers, chosen on a cross community basis. All are referred from the statutory agencies as being 'at risk'. They are chosen from a waiting list of some 70-90 families each year. One of the unique features of the work is that it is based on attendance for a period of one year. The first eight months the groups meet on two days per week. Following a residential experience at the Corrymeela Centre, the groups attend on one day for the remaining four months. The reason for this structure is to encourage the mothers to foster an independence from the Cottage and to develop self belief and self confidence when they leave. Support does continue after this and staff visit families in their own homes when requested. During the morning children under 5 are cared for in the crèche and playground. There is a weekly after-school club for the primary school children of mothers who attend one of the groups.

Grant McCullough took up the post in 1988 as the first full-time Co-ordinator at the Cottage. This was the beginning of a commitment by Grant to the present day. Together with a dedicated group of staff and volunteers he has created a haven: a place where mothers find acceptance, love and care; a place to rediscover their confidence and self worth and to face the future with their children. There are many records of the mothers' comments over the past 20 years. Among them:

> *'When I came to Quaker Cottage I thought there was no hope for me.... Now a year on I've changed beyond belief.... I can look to the future now with confidence and that I have one. My children can see a future too....'*
> *UQSC Annual Report 07/08* '

> *It changed me because I learnt self-respect'*

> *'They showed me love big-time'*

> *(Both Bischoff, C.D. 2006)*

The self-respect mothers gain impacts on the life of their children. The most common answer given by mothers when asked *'did your time at Quaker Cottage affect your parenting?'* was expressed as the feeling that they were able to understand their children better and see more clearly how their actions, as a parent, impact on their children.

Two other activities have become regular features of life at Quaker Cottage. Each Christmas an appeal goes out to all local Quaker Meetings and Friends School, Lisburn for help with food and gifts for the families involved in the Cottage work. Around 100 boxes of food are collected and distributed just prior to Christmas. This is deeply appreciated and helps over what can be a difficult period for many mothers who manage on a very small income. The other provision is the summer scheme when up to 200 school-age children come for full-day activities over several weeks of the school holidays.

Teenagers and the Troubles

In 1999 the needs of young people with relatives in prison were brought to the Committee. There was a concern that often these young people serve a 'silent sentence' because of the loss of an important family member and its effect on family life and on the individual young person. There were many such young people in communities where paramilitary groups had a strong influence at this time. With the aid of a major grant from the Princess Diana Memorial Fund, a 3-year project commenced in the evenings and at weekends at the Cottage for a group of young people from these backgrounds.

From the start there were difficulties and the project never succeeded in reaching its potential. After significant efforts were made to develop the work and an independent evaluation, the Committee closed the project in June 2003. It was regrettable that such important work could not be sustained. However, it was a valuable experience and when the Cottage staff proposed a new scheme for teenagers at risk later in 2003 it was agreed to proceed.

By the late 1990s, Cottage staff had created an ad hoc programme to cater for the 13-15 age group, now attending the after-school activities in increasing numbers. This was becoming increasingly difficult to run, with growing demand and without a qualified youth worker. A successful application was made to the Northern Ireland Executive's Children's Fund (NIECF) for funding to enable a properly staffed teenage project to begin. The project was designed to provide an opportunity for the teenage children of the families who were currently, or had in the past, been referred to the Cottage to gain valuable life skills and develop a sense of purpose. The values of elementary morality, personal well being of mind and body and the concept of self worth were to be promoted.

The project engaged young people who were vulnerable and at risk from substance misuse, crime and anti-social behaviour, parental conflict, low educational achievement and poor physical and emotional health among other difficulties. The areas they lived in presented a higher than average number of teen suicides. Drinking, drug abuse and underage sexual relations were much more prevalent than almost anywhere else in the UK or Ireland. Over 50% of the young people attending would be considered disabled, mainly with hidden impairments such as Attention Deficit Hyperactivity Disorder, Asperger's Syndrome, Dyslexia and similar neurological difficulties.

The project has been running successfully since 2003 with as many as 60 young men and women up to 18 years of age attending each year. The records speak for themselves with an attendance rate of over 85% which is virtually unknown in most other youth provisions in the area. A creative programme is provided to engage these young people, many of whom are outside of school or any other youth facility, and helping to build an atmosphere of trust and respect. Sessions include group work, discussion and activities as well as one-to-one counseling sessions and home visits. The teenage project was externally evaluated in 2007. The evaluation report stated:

> *'It is clear that the level and quality of engagement with some very vulnerable, challenging and marginalised young people that this project achieves should be the envy of many similar projects. Indeed the nature and quality of this work should be celebrated and promoted as an example of good practice'.*
>
> *Yiasouma, K. 2007*

This work took time to build but gradually has become an established part of the Cottage programme. It was made possible by an annual grant from NIECF. Unfortunately this will be stopped in 2009 and without further funding this important intervention with a group of young people from the local communities will have to be terminated. The Management Board have continued to press a number of Government sources to recognise the importance of this work for young people and their future.

3. THE CRIMINAL JUSTICE SYSTEM

From the earliest years of the prison work the Committee and staff have felt the need to influence policy and practice. Obviously the prison regime was the central concern but there were times when Friends brought issues of major concern to the Government's attention, partly to inform but also to persuade of the need for a change in policy. Within the prison system this often ranged across very practical areas like the provision of a canteen/waiting area to the development of family visits within the Prison. The Committee has sought to work with the prison authorities in a spirit of partnership, sharing concerns, encouraging good practice and promoting Northern Ireland prisons as being innovative and having high professional standards in the work with prisoners and their families.

Restorative Justice

The 25th Anniversary of the work of the Committee was celebrated in 1994. That year was also 'International Year of the

Child'. To mark both events the Committee agreed to explore the potential of Restorative Justice within the criminal justice system. This is an alternative to the retributive system of punishment for criminal behaviour. It is based on the belief that a better outcome can be achieved for the victim, the offender and the local community by bringing the victim and the offender together. It provides an opportunity for the victims to describe the pain and feelings of loss and for the offender to appreciate the distress, to acknowledge the wrongdoing and to seek forgiveness. It offers the offender the support he/she needs to try and make good the harm done and to seek help. For the victim, it provides the recognition of the hurt and sometimes the opportunity to be part of the solution.

By the early 1990s, restorative justice practice and philosophy was attracting interest across many sectors of the community in Northern Ireland. UQSC organised a conference to bring together people concerned with or working in criminal justice and to provide an opportunity for information sharing. The people who attended ranged across judges, police, prison service and agencies involved in preventative work. At this time there were no restorative justice schemes in Northern Ireland. Many of those involved with the justice system were struggling with young people in persistent trouble with the law. For most of the participants it:

'laid out new ideas, indeed a whole new way of thinking about justice in society'.

UQSC Annual Report 1994

The conference was highly successful and a report was produced which was to make an important contribution to the development of restorative justice in the years since. As a direct outcome of the conference, the Restorative Justice Working Group NI was formed. Its aim was to inform those connected with the criminal justice system about restorative justice and to establish restorative justice as an integral part of that system and not just as an adjunct to it. From the beginning the Group, chaired by Vincent Bent, by now Director of UQSC, had representation across the statutory and voluntary sectors and has maintained contact with government and community-based restorative justice groups, the judiciary and the police. When the Government decided to promote this alternative approach, the Northern Ireland Office established a Restorative Justice Steering Group and some members from the

Working Group were invited to become members. The Review of the Criminal Justice System in Northern Ireland (2000) made a recommendation for the development of restorative justice approaches for juvenile offenders. The principle was accepted by the Government and provisions were made in the Justice (NI) Act 2002 for youth conferences.

New Legislation

The Group organised a follow-up conference ten years later in 2004 to take stock and draw attention to the dramatic changes in restorative justice in Northern Ireland. This included the implementation of the Criminal Justice Review and work done by the Police and community restorative justice groups. The conference report stated:

> *'The province can be proud of its indigenous restorative justice practice. There remain tensions regarding policy issues and who should have responsibility and oversight. However, great encouragement can be taken from the fact that as time moves, relationships between the protagonists are being shaped and for the most part, in very constructive ways'.*
>
> *Conference Report 2004*

In 2005, the Group changed its name to the Restorative Justice Forum (RJF) to reflect a change in emphasis, acknowledging that the day-to-day work was now being done by a number of organisations and that the group's future role would lie in networking, promotion and learning. The Forum's terms of reference state:

> *'The first ten years of the group's work owes a great deal to the commitment and energy of the first Chair Vincent Bent, and the support of Ulster Quaker Service Committee'.*
>
> *RJF 2005*

The Forum continues to promote restorative justice by providing an independent, neutral space in which restorative justice philosophy, practice and developments can be explored. Learning continues to be promoted through seminars, conferences, research and the dissemination of information. Local Friends have continued to support this work over the past 14 years and have been active in supporting regional forums and in promoting interest and innovation with both the criminal justice agencies and with victims' organizations.

THE EVOLUTION OF UQSC

It is doubtful if those Friends who formed the original Emergency Committee ever imagined that some 40 years on it would still be here and playing such a positive role in working for peace and social justice. Friends have demonstrated that although small in number, they are led by their spiritual convictions to reach out to those in need, no matter what their background or beliefs. However, if the work was to continue from these early emergency responses there needed to be some structure and organisation to provide a platform for planning and delivering services. Creating and maintaining an organisation 'fit for purpose' together with ensuring its financial viability have been the two main tenets of the charity since UQSC was formed in 1972.

No organisation is without its challenges and difficulties and Quaker Service is no exception. It has been fortunate in having a committee (and now a management board) made up of like-minded people, members and attenders of the Society of Friends and those who are in sympathy with the ethos of a Quaker faith-based charity. That is not suggesting that everything has run smoothly over the past 40 years. It is an organisation made up of people with differing ideas and aspirations. New services brought about challenges to the way the charity was organised and managed. Change is difficult for most people and Quakers are no exception. From time to time a number of features not uncommon in the development of a voluntary organization needed to be confronted however uncomfortable. The list below gives a flavour of the kind of issues faced over the 40 years. The committee developed as a result of the pain as well as the success:

- Disagreement within the committee over crucial decisions on the way forward which led to a rare resignation
- Disagreement between committee and staff and between senior staff as to delegated authority, roles and responsibilities
- Fall-off in committee membership, especially from Friends outside the Greater Belfast area, at times leading to concerns as to the sustainability as a Quaker organisation

- Occasional difficulties in recruiting staff with expertise and in sympathy with the ethos of the work
- The shift from a volunteer organisation to a professional statutory-regulated agency
- The need for greater clarity about governance (This emerged during the 80s and 90s, when UQSC needed to continually re-examine and renew its arrangements. The commitment by the Committee to take time out every year or two to review its work and acknowledge the need for change became important here.)

FUNDING THE WORK

The development of services over these years has been made possible by the support of Friends across the world who have responded in so many ways but crucially with their financial support. It has been uplifting and supportive to have these gifts from Quaker meetings, individuals and trusts to sustain the work and it would not have been possible to survive without this help. In addition the statutory agencies have regarded the work of Quakers with respect and integrity and over the years their support has been the financial backbone of the work both in the prisons and in the community. However, even with this support, by the 1990s the Committee faced considerable financial pressures each year.

Following a suggestion by the Director, some research was carried out as to the possibility of a charity shop. The decision was taken to form a trading company, Quaker Care. The main purpose was to provide financial support for Quaker Service; opportunities to volunteer, and to raise the profile of the charity. With the help of Quaker trusts a building was purchased on the Lisburn Road, Belfast and the first shop opened in 1998. The building provided an opportunity for permanent office accommodation. Later in 2001 a second shop opened on the Woodstock Road, Belfast. Both shops offer two important contributions. They provide a valuable source of income and also the opportunity for Friends and others to volunteer. The shops are doing well and the Woodstock Road shop provides a unique opportunity to reach out and support a number of ethnic minority communities who live in the area.

More recently, the Committee needed to improve its core funding from the two major statutory funders, the Northern Ireland

Prison Service and the Belfast Health & Social Care Trust. In 2004/5 the Prison Service decided that all major services in the prison would have to be tendered. This presented Quakers with the unique challenge of having to tender for a range of services all of which they started in the first place! However UQSC was awarded a contract in 2006 for 5 years and the financial settlement was a considerable improvement on the previous funding.

From the earliest days of the Cottage work the Committee has had to rely heavily on contributions from Friends and charities. The grant from the local Health & Social Services Trust did not cover all the costs. In 2005 a concerted effort was made by staff and committee to convince the authorities of the financial pressures facing the work. The present Director organised a series of meetings with senior managers from the Trust. The evidence of the need together with the acknowledgement of the high level of services provided by the Cottage persuaded the Trust to substantially increase its annual grant.

THE FUTURE – A NEW DIRECTOR AND A LIMITED COMPANY

2004 saw the beginning of a number of important changes in the life of UQSC. It was with great sadness the Committee said farewell to Vincent Bent who had led the organisation through some very difficult times. With his vision and enthusiasm he encouraged the Committee and the staff to innovate and respond to needs as they emerged and supported staff as they faced continual pressures at the prison and the Cottage. It was not surprising that he decided after 25 years to have a well-earned rest. His successor, Janette McKnight, was appointed in February 2005. With the new Director, the Committee determined to examine the fitness of the organisation to face the challenges and opportunities of the next few years. Two particular features emerged which required urgent attention. The first was a concern regarding the legal position of the voluntary committee members. New expectations and demands were being made of voluntary sector boards and it was essential to provide them with better protection and support. With the help of Ulster Quarterly Meeting a consultative process was undertaken which resulted in the decision to become a limited company. Assurance was given that the new agency would always remain a Quaker charity governed by Ulster Friends. The legal change was made to form a limited company in March 2007. This provided the opportunity to modernize its image and structures, to rename the agency 'Quaker Service' and to create a positive and helpful publicity campaign.

Staff and Volunteers

UQSC had grown by 2005 to become a middle range regulated agency with an annual budget of £600,000, employing 40 full-time and part-time staff. This is a significant change from its foundation and the early years which involved an immediate response to practical needs. As the work grew in both the prison and the family centre, it became increasingly important to ensure trained and qualified staff were available to develop longer term plans. This has not removed the opportunity for volunteers to remain active. The Cottage provides the opportunity for young full-time volunteers from America and Europe for periods of 1-2 years. The Summer Scheme attracts a number of young local volunteers. The opening of the two shops has encouraged some 30 Quakers and others to give some time each week. The development of a number of new initiatives for prisoner support at Maghaberry will provide the opportunity to recruit and train a further team of volunteers.

Whilst there have been difficulties from time to time, the organization has been very fortunate in the calibre and quality of the staff it recruits. There are no Quakers among the current staff group. A number of the staff have been working for Quaker Service (and previously UQSC) for many years which gives a very clear indication of their commitment and loyalty to the agency. Without exception all have demonstrated in their commitment and care their acceptance of the Quaker Ethos* in the work.

CONCLUSIONS

The improved financial position has given the new Management Board and Director of Quaker Service the confidence and capacity to begin to explore new opportunities within the prison and in the community. Work is actively underway in developing a number of new projects within Maghaberry. Contact has been made with the women's prison at Hydebank and some developmental work has started.

* Quaker Ethos – based on values as described in Chapter 1.

The Cottage continues to reach out to the needs of many families in North and West Belfast. There remains so much unmet need within the City of Belfast. For many families, particularly single parents living on a low income, the pressures can cause all types of breakdown. The work at the Cottage has shown that a loving, caring and therapeutic environment can relieve the stress and give mothers the confidence to face the future with their children. The big questions being considered by Quaker Service now are: How to provide the opportunity for other families not in the present catchment area? To remain as a single model of good practice or to grow? These provide exciting and challenging opportunities for Friends.

Independent research in 2006 on the work of Quaker Cottage found:

'...the feedback from the women and referrers was over whelmingly positive, a sign that although the project is small, it is making a significant impact on the lives of those it touches'.

Bischoff, C.D. 2006

This captures the basis for all that Ulster Friends have tried to do over the past 40 years. There is no claim to have had a significant impact on the political situation in Northern Ireland, but rather a quiet interface with many individuals and families. Friends' belief in 'that of God in everyone' has been the foundation of a Quaker ethos which has permeated the work of all the staff and volunteers over these years. It is the value and worth Friends place on each individual. It is this ethos that has become the unique feature of a culture of care and acceptance at both Quaker Cottage and Maghaberry Prison. Whatever the future holds for Northern Ireland, Quakers will continue to work for peace and social justice, believing that, with God's help, the divided communities can find reconciliation and build a society based on acceptance and respect for each other.

References

Belfast Friends Emergency Committee Minutes 1969.

Bischoff, C.D. (2006) **They Showed Me Love Big Time: An Exploration of the Work and Impact of Quaker**

Cottage in Northern Ireland MA Dissertation University of Bradford.

RJF Restorative Justice Forum **Terms of Reference 2005.**

Restorative Justice Group NI **Conference Report 2004.**

UQM Ulster Quarterly Meeting **Minutes 1969.**

UQSC Ulster Quaker Service Committee/Quaker Service: **Annual Reports 1980-2009.**

UQSC Ulster Quaker Service Committee/Quaker Service **Minutes September 1969 - December 2008.**

Yiasouma, K. (2007) **Evaluation of Quaker Cottage Teenage Programme:** internal document: undertaken by Include Youth.

Chapter 4

THE CENTRE FOR NEIGHBOURHOOD DEVELOPMENT

David Bass

'By involving people in the affairs which touch their everyday lives, they can gain self-assurance and can look more clearly at the conflict within their society and at constructive solutions to their problems.'
CfND Annual Report 1975

THIS CHAPTER will examine the work of the Centre for Neighbourhood Development (CfND) throughout its 15 years, its legacy and some of the lessons learned. The initial Quaker influence shaped the way the organisation worked in a variety of ways such as the use of consensus decision making, the commitment to being cross community, the involvement of workers on the management committee and a flat pay structure. Although the Quaker involvement in the organisation was strongest in the initial stages, these practices continued until the organisation closed through lack of funding in 1992.

CfND employed local neighbourhood workers in the Greater Belfast area from 1975 to 1992. The idea came from discussions among a number of Friends and other people involved in community work in Belfast in the early 1970s. Although it started out with two Friends as staff, a base in the Friends Institute in Belfast and a committee made up largely of Friends in 1975, it was never formally part of the Religious Society of Friends. As the organisation grew it employed neighbourhood workers in six areas of Belfast on both sides of the political divide, i.e. in both Catholic and Protestant areas. The project was experimental both in the work carried out and in the way the organisation was run. It was an important influence on the development of neighbourhood community work in Belfast and played a major role in developing practical ideas such as local health and community economic development projects. At that time it was a unique cross community organisation working in areas of the city where there were strong paramilitary influences.

BACKGROUND AND ORIGINS

The first discussions on the CfND project started in early 1974. At this stage in the history of Northern Ireland internment without trial had been in place for nearly three years; there was significant civil unrest and violence including Bloody Sunday in 1972 and frequent bombings such as the Bloody Friday bombings when over 20 bombs exploded in one afternoon in the Belfast area. At the beginning of 1974 the power-sharing Executive was set up as part of the Sunningdale Agreement but during May the Ulster Workers' Council strike brought much of Northern Ireland to a standstill and caused the collapse of the Executive (McKay 2000).

While CfND's origins are linked to this social and political unrest they are more closely linked with the Northern Ireland Community Relations Commission (NICRC), which was set up in 1970 as part of Prime Minister Jim Callaghan's package for dealing with Northern Ireland. The NICRC was modelled on the Race Relations Commission in Britain. At a talk at CfND's first Annual Conference in November 1975, Maurice Hayes, first chairman of NICRC, explained the difficulties they had from the beginning because of the unrealistic expectations for the body to bring Catholics and Protestants together. He said that at an early stage, because of the awareness of the great social needs of communities, NICRC decided to work to develop separate communities and then consider mutual problems using broad issues such as housing and transport. The NICRC was independent of Government, although it had to report to Parliament annually. A team of 17 or so Community Development Workers were employed, based in Belfast, Dungannon and Derry*. However the community devel-

---

* Also known as Londonderry.

opment work and the resultant community infrastructure brought the NICRC into conflict with the Ministry of Community Relations who felt its role was being usurped, and in April 1974 the Northern Ireland Executive's Minister of Community Relations, Ivan Cooper, announced that the NICRC was to be wound up (Chapter 7 section on Community Development).

Felicity McCartney, a local Friend, and Lisa Huber*, an American Friend, were both employed by NICRC as Community Development Workers in East Belfast. Once the decision was taken to make their team redundant, they started work with others on ideas for continuing the community development work in which they had been engaged. This led to the establishment of CfND.

QUAKER INVOLVEMENT

CfND had strong Quaker associations though it was not an official Quaker project. Paul Cadbury's article 'Official and Unofficial Quaker Service' discusses the Friends Ambulance Unit, described as being:

> *'as much in the tradition of Quaker Service as anything which was done through the Society's own appointed machinery. But to the last the unit was constitutionally independent, nor can the Society of Friends be responsible for what it did'.*

Cadbury, Paul S.

Using the Northern Ireland examples, he talks about the work being done at the Maze Prison as official work and the work undertaken by CfND and at the Frederick Street Project, the forerunner of Quaker House, as unofficial.

A committee was set up drawing together Friends and people with community work experience, in roughly equal numbers. Friends or attenders of Quaker meetings held all the committee offices initially and provided the four trustees. The project was first housed in the Friends Institute building, adjacent to Frederick Street Meeting House and was seen as complementary to the Frederick Street Project. Many of the principles and methods of working had a strong Quaker influence and even the initial sources of money were mainly Quaker charitable trusts, but this

---

* Now Ann Le Mare.

was to diversify later. By 1978 there were still five Quakers out of the 12 committee members. During that year Felicity and Lisa left at different times and after that no Friends were employed by the project and the Quaker influence declined.

However the project was an ambitious and specialised one and brought in many other influences from the broad community work field. It aimed to recruit local neighbourhood workers and give representation on the management committee to people from the local areas where they worked. Rowntree and Cadbury* were still major funders, but from 1978 there was a substantial amount of statutory funding from Belfast City Council. During 1980 CfND moved its office from the Friends Institute, although Annual Meetings continued to be held at Frederick Street Meeting House. By 1982 there was only one attender involved in the project. That remained the position until the project closed ten years later. Given that most of the Quaker influence was at the initial period, this chapter concentrates on the early years of CfND, although mention is made of later developments and issues as well as the legacy of the first few years.

SETTING UP THE PROJECT

The start of CfND is well documented. Discussion papers were prepared from mid-1974 onward and, from these, the aims and objectives of the project evolved. In the initial proposal four reasons were put forward for the project. One was the demise of the NICRC and a second was the expressed desire for workers in specific communities. The other two were Quaker reasons. One was for a community work project to act in a complementary way to the Frederick Street Project, which worked at a political level. The other was headed 'The Quaker Contribution' and described as follows:

'Quakers have a tradition of responding to situations of conflict. They are in a position in Northern Ireland at present of being acceptable to a wide variety of people across religious and class barriers. Their workers could bring a wide perspective to the work, drawing on the experience of other Quaker work as well as other community work'.

Huber & McCartney 1974

* Joseph Rowntree Charitable Trust and Barrow and Geraldine Cadbury Trust.

64

The proposal was always to have a Central Office supporting a limited number of community workers working in small well-defined areas. The first discussion paper also states that 'the work of the project would be based on Quaker principles of non-violence and providing alternatives to violent change through community development' (ibid). It went on to say:

'Community Development … is a process which enables individuals and communities to use their own talents and growth potential to create a society in which they have access to resources adequate to meet their needs.'

(ibid.)

The discussion papers always referred to a project committee made up of Friends and others including area representatives. During the summer of 1974 proposals were circulated to a number of community development experts for their views. Encouraged by the letters of support received in response, work started on its community work policy, its constitution, setting up the committee and finding the necessary finance.

1 The aims of the project were finalised by November 1974 and guided CfND for the whole 15 years of its life. They were:
2 To assist communities to effect fundamental change for the good of society.
3 To actively encourage participation in and shared responsibility for those resources and institutions which structure our society.
4 To relate these institutions and agencies to the needs of communities and to foster cooperation between the communities and the agencies which serve them.
5 To provide a base for the training of community workers and for the dissemination of information.
6 To promote research and evaluation into the methods and philosophy of community development and any other relevant areas.
7 To demonstrate to the statutory agencies in Northern Ireland the need for neighbourhood/community work and to show that it is as necessary as any form of community care and to encourage government support.
8 To promote formal and informal education as an integral part of the community development programme.

At the same time as the aims were being developed, guidelines were being drawn up for the community development work which was to 'provide alternatives to violent change' (CfND Community Work Policy 1974). Community workers would be involved in five broad activities:

1 The promotion of an awareness and understanding of individual and community needs and of the means through which these can be identified.
2 The identification and development of resources to help meet these needs.
3 The growth of confidence and ability of communities to tackle their problems through self help.
4 Encouraging local leadership to work with their communities in determining their needs and to ensure that resources are made available to them.
5 Promoting awareness on the part of statutory agencies that people have a right to be involved in the way services are provided and to participate in the sharing of resources.

While the objectives of the project were being finalised, the practicalities of setting up an organisation were also being tackled. A constitution was prepared and changed gradually to suit the needs of the project. After some deliberation the name 'Centre for Neighbourhood Development' was chosen. Membership of the committee was to be drawn from three sources: members of South Belfast and Frederick Street Friends Meetings; representatives from the communities in which CfND had employed workers; and people with special skills and interests. Having representatives from neighbourhoods was very unusual at the time, as there were limited opportunities for community group members to be involved in wider organisations and personal safety was often a consideration where people moved outside their immediate community. The aim was to have a project which would not be delivered by people from outside the neighbourhoods but rather for local communities to run their own programmes with outside support and advice where needed.

Although not unique to Quakers, an interesting and significant variation to the normal workings of committees was the attendance of paid workers at all committee meetings, taking part in all decisions except those affecting their own appointment. This policy continued for the whole time CfND was in existence and at times caused difficulties. For instance when CfND became a limited company it was not permissible for paid staff to be Directors. However, the Directors were able to delegate all day-to-day decisions to a committee which included the paid workers.

INFORMAL BEGINNINGS

The first meeting of the steering committee was held in October 1974 when five new members joined. The first activity was that the new members 'were introduced to each other' (CfND Minutes 1974). This author was present at the first meeting and remained on the committee for the whole of the life of CfND, becoming the first Convenor of the committee in December 1974. At various times he served as Treasurer and Secretary and had a second period as Convenor starting in 1985. The committee met a further seven times before the end of 1974 by which time there was a total of twelve members. Frequent meetings were needed to set up premises and make arrangements for the employment of workers as early as possible in 1975.

By the end of the year finance had been offered by the Barrow and Geraldine S. Cadbury Trust and the Joseph Rowntree Charitable Trust. A further major funder – the Calouste Gulbenkian Foundation – was later found and, between the three trusts, CfND was able to raise over 90% of the £17,000 needed for the first year. Both Rowntree and Cadbury supported CfND for many years with Cadbury continuing until the mid-1980s. Over the years CfND received substantial amounts of money from Friends Meetings within Britain and Ireland and further afield as well as receiving large grants from a range of Quaker trusts and similar bodies. German Friends were particularly supportive mainly through Quakerhilfe.

Job descriptions for two central staff had been developed by the end of 1974. One was a Development Officer whose work concentrated on identifying potential project areas and working with the local communities on the employment and support of a community worker. The second post was a Training Officer who provided support to the neighbourhood workers and organised training for CfND staff and other community workers. Shared duties included research and evaluation, fund raising, working with statutory agencies and general project development. The committee also agreed to pay the central staff and the neighbourhood workers on the same salary scale so that there would be no hierarchy within the agency. This policy was continued throughout CfND's life and, in conjunction with the staff attendance at committee meetings, meant that CfND, due largely to the Quaker influence, remained an egalitarian organisation at a time when this was far from being a common practice.

THE INITIAL WORK AND THE NEIGHBOURHOODS

During December 1974 the committee agreed to appoint Lisa as Development Officer and Felicity as Training Officer starting from 1st January 1975. They moved quickly to appoint a part-time Secretary and the first Neighbourhood Community Worker, Danny Taggart, who was appointed for the Short Strand, an area already known to Lisa and Felicity from their work in East Belfast. CfND quickly realised that it needed a clear rationale for the selection of areas where workers would be appointed. Selection had to be careful for a range of reasons not the least being the intention to employ only six neighbourhood workers where there were far more than six potential areas. Following detailed research and careful consideration the committee used these criteria for selection of neighbourhoods to ensure variety and balance:

1. Areas which showed different types of social problems;
2. Where the development of the community is at different stages;
3. And which show a wide geographical spread;
4. Where there are no similar workers;
5. Where the need for a neighbourhood worker has been expressed by the community;
6. Where there are active people who would benefit from employment by the project.

By early 1978 six areas had been selected and six neighbourhood workers employed. During the three years taken to select these six, a number of other areas were considered but not selected. Some areas in both Protestant East and Catholic West Belfast were considered but not accepted, either because there was not enough community support or because they already had a worker appointed in a broadly similar role. A mixed community in

South Belfast was considered but not selected because the local association was considered strong enough to employ its own worker. One of the later decisions was to select one of two Catholic estates in West Belfast. Both of these areas would have been suitable but would have been too similar and close together to appoint a worker in each. In the end, the one with the least community facilities was selected.

1. Short Strand

Danny Taggart started working as a Neighbourhood Community Worker in Short Strand in January 1975. He lived in the area and was already working as a voluntary community worker. Short Strand was an interesting area for CfND to select first. It was a mainly Catholic area of around 3,000 people situated immediately to the east of the river Lagan and surrounded on the other three sides by Protestant areas with resultant sectarian tensions. The community was faced by issues of poverty and unemployment, but was also under physical threat from people in the neighbouring areas and from plans for a ring road. The housing in the area all dated from the 19th century and was due for redevelopment. Danny was therefore faced with a wide range of challenges.

One of his first steps was to help acquire a community centre for the area. Appropriately for a Quaker project, the building acquired had previously been a pub and was given a new role! The St. Matthews Community Centre soon became a focus for activities for all sections of the Short Strand community. Activities included a senior citizens club, social evenings, youth activities, films, adult education classes, keep fit sessions and community meetings. The building also provided a base for summer playschemes.

In a separate development, Danny established an advice centre in a house he used as an office. He was assisted in the centre by local residents who had been trained in giving advice on the many problems faced by the community. Housing and redevelopment, welfare rights and security issues proved a major focus both for Danny and the centre. He was frequently called upon to help with issues relating to security including bomb damage and the results of shootings. Law students were also brought in to help give advice on many of the issues facing Short Strand residents. This link with university students arranged through the recently established Belfast Law

Centre was a good example of the way CfND was able to link the neighbourhoods with useful external bodies who could assist in the local areas.

However, the main focus of activity was on housing. Danny helped establish a Tenants Association to act as the focal point for discussion with the Housing Executive* on redevelopment plans for the area. There were two particular successes for Danny in this field. Firstly he helped set up the St. Matthews Housing Association which from 1977 took responsibility for the improvement of housing in a Housing Action Area in the heart of Short Strand. Secondly he played a key role in securing the relocation of a major factory from the centre of the area to the edge thus making a substantial amount of land available for housing, ensuring that sufficient new dwellings were provided for the community in the redevelopment process. These two steps were critical in securing the long-term future of the Short Strand community.

2. Lower Oldpark

The second area selected for a Neighbourhood Community Worker, Lower Oldpark, had many similarities with Short Strand but also significant differences. It is a largely Protestant area in North Belfast and, unlike Short Strand, it was seen as an area in decline with an older population and many bricked-up houses. As an area of older housing with few facilities, it was facing redevelopment. One of the significant differences for CfND was that the worker appointed in the area, Betty Rice, was not a local resident but came from another Protestant community. Unlike Danny, therefore, Betty had to get to know the local community before she could make a significant contribution to the area.

Betty started work in August 1975 and immediately became involved in the local summer playscheme. Following this she carried out a survey of the area to acquaint herself with the community and the various social issues it faced. She was particularly concerned about the number of isolated older people and quickly became involved in arranging activities for this age group. These included lunch clubs, outings and a pensioners' club. In 1976 Betty obtained the use of a disused shop which became both her base and a centre for adult and youth activities as well as an advice centre.

---

* NI Housing Executive – The Housing Authority covering all of Northern Ireland.

As in Short Strand, the redevelopment process took up a lot of Betty's time in the early years but most of her time was spent in establishing, supporting and working with local groups and committees. She helped ensure that the local primary school remained open and carried out a lot of work to provide activities for young people including playschemes, youth clubs and playgroups.

3. Lower Shankill

The third neighbourhood selected, Lower Shankill, a Protestant area in West Belfast, was a new estate mainly consisting of flats and maisonettes facing many social problems. The Lower Shankill estate was part of the overall Shankill area where there was considerable community activity but it was one of the more unsettled parts of the area largely as a result of the unpopular blocks of flats. Shankill interfaces with several Catholic areas and wider sectarian tension was a continual background to the work. Dan Godfrey was appointed early in 1976. His initial study of the area revealed a lack of activities for adults. As a result Dan arranged a series of adult education classes on pottery, car maintenance and welfare rights. He acted as co-ordinator for a summer playscheme, supported the existing community centre and set up a new neighbourhood centre in another part of the area, basing his office there.

The Lower Shankill differed from the other two CfND areas in that it was part of a bigger community. Dan worked with a number of groups involved in the wider Shankill area, in many cases on wider projects which involved the Lower Shankill estate. He organised adult education classes and worked in local youth clubs as well as organising holidays which helped to link young people from Lower Shankill to wider networks, some of them cross community.

4. New Lodge

The fourth neighbourhood, New Lodge, was very much at CfND's back door as it was the area adjoining Frederick Street. New Lodge was a largely Catholic area of some 10,000 people with a mixture of older housing and multi-storey flats. The area was diverse with many different factions. The multi-storey flats were unpopular but the area as a whole had a very high demand for housing and there was little scope for redeveloping the older housing. Like Lower Oldpark it was a part of North Belfast which suffered significantly from inter-community strife. It was significantly larger in terms of population than the first three areas and as a result the worker appointed, Seamus McAloran, was able to become involved in a wider range of activities. Seamus initially concentrated on meeting the various active groups in the area and on the housing issues in the Housing Action Area where the Housing Executive was engaged in a major programme to improve living conditions in an area of older housing. Early on he helped set up a film club, two lunch clubs and a Mother and Toddlers group.

Seamus always carried out a lot of work with young people. He established a football club and gave considerable support to existing youth groups. He was able to establish a base in a house shared with the Housing Executive in the Housing Action Area and used it as a contact point for staff from various statutory agencies working in the area.

5. Twinbrook

Unlike the first four areas Twinbrook was not an inner city area nor was it in the Belfast City Council area. It was a new housing estate of some 7,000 people on the fringe of West Belfast and was within the Lisburn District Council area. While it had originally been established as an experimental mixed community, by the time CfND appointed a worker it had become almost entirely Catholic. Like New Lodge it was a larger community with a wide range of social problems. Many of the issues in Twinbrook concerned the establishment of a new community with little existing social cohesion, few facilities and a very high proportion of children and young families.

Lilian McManus was appointed in September 1977 and quickly got to know the wide range of community groups working in the area. Much of her initial work was with children with an emphasis on securing facilities for pre-school activities. Lilian worked to develop adult education classes in the area and provided assistance to various groups including a Sports Association, the Tenants Association and a Housing Action Group. The latter groups dealt with issues such as problems with the district heating system and the lack of a health centre in the area while the Sports Association worked for the provision of sports facilities for young people in the area.

6. Cregagh

The final area selected was different again. Cregagh was a well-established housing estate in outer East Belfast. It was probably the most stable area selected since the community, which was largely Protestant, had been established for over 20 years and did not face the sorts of special problems like sectarian interfaces or redevelopment faced by the other CfND areas. Like Twinbrook, it was outside the Belfast City boundary, in this case in the Castlereagh Council area. The worker appointed, Jim Gregg, started work early in 1978. He had the advantage of already being involved in running the local community centre and was able to use it as a base from the beginning.

In the early months Jim developed the use of the centre and organised a summer playscheme. He established contact with the Probation Service so that they were able to use the Centre to work with their young people. Jim was able to establish a range of activities in the Centre, including a Senior Citizens Day Centre and a playscheme for 5-10 year olds. He helped develop a successful Tenants Association separate from the management committee of the centre.

Area Representatives

One of the aims of CfND was that each of the areas should be represented on the management committee. This proved problematic in some cases. It worked well for Short Strand where Danny was able to recommend a colleague from the adjoining Markets area, Hugh Leatham, who became a core member of the committee and in due course became its Convenor. Eddie Meneally became the Lower Oldpark representative and was an active committee member until he moved away and subsequently left the committee. Fergus Derby represented the New Lodge but did not become a regular attender, although he was heavily involved with the work Seamus and other CfND staff carried out in the area. While a representative from Lower Shankill was on the committee for a short time, CfND was never able to find suitable people from the other areas.

TRAINING

One of the core benefits of CfND as an organisation was that it enabled individual community workers to learn from each other and to take part in relevant training programmes. CfND was unusual at the time in the emphasis it gave to the provision of training. In particular it encouraged local workers with limited academic qualifications to pursue studies at university level. The first two neighbourhood workers enrolled on University of Ulster's in-service Youth and Community Work certificate course. Considerable support was also given to adult education within the neighbourhoods (Huber & McCartney 1980).

Each time a new worker started, an induction programme was organised. This also served as a refresher course for existing workers. The initial course, provided primarily for Danny Taggart, had a concentrated week of discussions, visits etc. and continued with weekly events right through to the summer of 1975. It included visits to an Advice Centre, the Voluntary Service Bureau, Corrymeela, a community-based adult education programme, an adventure playground and various community work projects; seminars on environmental health services, keeping accounts and counselling; and discussions with staff in Social Services, the Housing Executive, Social Security and the Workers Education Association. In other words it was a comprehensive briefing on a wide range of issues relevant to the work of a community worker.

When Betty Rice started in September 1975 a three-week programme was run. The aims of this programme were:

- To discuss ideas, issues and problems in relation to community work;
- To learn about specific projects in the community and meet the people working on them;
- To familiarise staff with the services provided by various statutory and voluntary agencies; and
- To help Betty get to know the Lower Oldpark area.

Each of the three weeks had a specific theme and this programme provided the basic format for future induction programmes:

1. Housing and redevelopment;
2. Play, youth and community centres; and
3. Statutory and voluntary social services.

Training sessions were not confined to induction programmes. Regular sessions were organised in Frederick Street and frequent visits were arranged to other projects. In the first year the most significant trip was a visit to Derry by staff and committee members. This included a visit to the Ballyarnett/Shantallow Resource Centre and a meeting with the editor of the 'Community Mirror' to discuss how to set up and run a community newspaper. During 1976 topics for staff discussion sessions included group work, legislation a community worker needs to understand, the use of video in community work and housing improvement.

The lack of similar training programmes for community workers in Belfast at the time led to the events being extended to community workers employed by other agencies. One example of this was a regular weekly film session where short films on community issues were used as a starting point for discussion sessions. This programme started in 1975 and developed in 1978 into a three-day film and video festival showing some mainstream films as well as community-produced videos including ones on Divis Flats, Corrymeela and Gingerbread. Each film was introduced by a speaker and followed by a discussion. Feature films shown included 'Kes', 'One Flew Over the Cuckoo's Nest' and 'Diary of a Mad Housewife'.

More extensive programmes were also run. For example in 1977 an eight-week evening class was organised on 'Running a Community Centre'. This course was attended by twenty-seven people from a total of sixteen groups. Topics covered included working with young people, activities for adults, finance and the role of a management committee. A two-day course was also organised on Supplementary Benefits* and later the same year one on 'Housing and Redevelopment', with around thirty people attending the full-day seminar held on a Saturday. In the morning presentations were given on case studies of three Belfast redevelopment areas by local community leaders and in the afternoon a series of workshops was organised on rehabilitation, redevelopment and organising for action.

One of the most ambitious events organised in CfND's early years was a two-day trip to Dublin arranged in conjunction with Geoffrey Corry of the National Youth Council and Senator Mary Robinson, the future Irish President. Sixteen people went on the

---

* A welfare benefit payment in UK at this time. 75

trip – eight from CfND and eight from other community and voluntary organisations. Many of these had never been to Dublin before. The group visited the Dail where they attended Question Time and had a discussion with Mary Robinson; the National Association of Tenants Associations; Ballyfermott Community Centre; the National Youth Council; and Artane Youth Club.

Closely linked to the training provided was work on Adult Education. In all the neighbourhoods there was some element of community-based adult education, emphasised as a core element of the project's work. At an early stage central staff developed close links with most of the Belfast-based adult education colleges as well as Queens University Belfast (QUB) and the Magee and Jordanstown campuses of the University of Ulster. They also had advice and support from Adam Curle, Professor of Peace Studies at Bradford University. The 1976 Annual Report stated that CfND's work in Community Education was at three levels:

1. The support and training of people working full time in the community work field;
2. The education of community groups and others involved in community action to help them achieve their aims; and
3. More general education of people in the community to help develop their interests and confidence.

An example of the link with the education establishments was a course on 'Your Pre-School Child' held for mothers by the QUB Extra Mural Department in three of the areas CfND was working in during 1976. A further example was a 10-week course held in the same year for people working in local advice centres on 'The Rights of Citizens' delivered by a Queens University Law lecturer. In 1977 a six-day course on 'Working in a Community' was organised by CfND central staff and delivered to 18 voluntary and full-time community workers in conjunction with the Workers Education Association (WEA). The following year a conference on Adult Education was organised in conjunction with the WEA.

ANNUAL CONFERENCES

CfND's experimental approach and emphasis on both training and evaluation led to it holding annual conferences for staff and committee members. The first of these was held in Bangor in November 1975 and established a pattern of events starting on a

Saturday morning and finishing on the Sunday afternoon. The conferences were thoroughly planned and often quite elaborate and were always well-attended. The first conference was attended by all five staff and by six committee members and provided guidance for the work in the coming year. There were four guest speakers:

1. Maurice Hayes, former Chairman of the Northern Ireland Community Relations Commission, who led a session entitled 'An Introduction to Community Development';
2. Professor Adam Curle who spoke on 'Community Work in a Violent Society' drawing on his knowledge of the 'Patans' of North West India and a large village in the Punjab;
3. Nicholas Ragg, a Lecturer in Social Studies at Surrey University (formerly at QUB) who discussed how to evaluate community work;
4. Donald Swift, Professor of Education at the Open University who led a session on 'Education and the Development of the Individual'.

The second Conference differed in that there were no external speakers. Instead four working groups of staff and committee members prepared for and led sessions on four themes which were to shape CfND work in 1977:

• Evaluation of Community Work;
• Grant Aid;
• Research; and
• The Structure of CfND.

The 1977 conference was attended by 15 people and looked largely at the way CfND was developing. At the end of the conference a series of decisions were taken about the methods used by the committee and about the future priorities for CfND. Conferences in later years were equally important in determining the future; for example, at the 1981 conference a decision was made that CfND should move into the field of community economic development. This formed a key focus of CfND's work during the 1980s and early 1990s (see below).

THE PROCESS OF EVALUATION

The committee had always taken the view that, since CfND was an experimental project in so many ways, it was important to ensure that the work was evaluated thoroughly, so it decided to undertake a major evaluation exercise in 1977, towards the end of the initial 3-year development phase. Like much of CfND's early work this was very experimental since major evaluations of this type were unusual at the time. A firm of consultants, ITS, some of whose partners were familiar with community development work and known to CfND staff, was engaged to undertake the evaluation. Most of the work was carried out on three separate Saturdays in the spring of 1977 where staff and committee members came together with an ITS consultant. ITS produced a report following these sessions and follow-up work took place in the autumn. This type of evaluation gradually became the norm for community and voluntary organisations, but CfND was very much a pioneer in using evaluation to shape the future direction of the organisation.

The first evaluation day focussed on separating out the different views of what was seen as the three groups within the project: the neighbourhood workers; the central staff; and the committee members. Each group looked at how the project's aims, resources, organisation and relationships had developed since the start and how they were likely to change in the future. To this mix was added the views of a number of people who were familiar with the work of the project. Some of these external views, which were not attributed to particular people, were interesting and sometimes controversial. There were, for instance, comments about there being too much Quaker influence, the use of consensus hiding conflict and policies being too vague. However there were also many very positive comments about the value of the work, the importance of training etc. One issue mentioned on several occasions was the potential for CfND to influence statutory agencies which did not appear to have been fulfilled.

The second day focussed on the experiences of Danny and Betty, the first two neighbourhood workers. Each described their area and then listed the achievements to date and showed their role in making these happen. From this and the ensuing discussion a chronological picture of community development appeared to emerge.

1. Conduct a survey, establish needs and priorities and develop a plan.
2. Build a network of contacts with individuals, groups and agencies.

3. Identify people who can and will do something.
4. Show opportunities and stimulate.
5. Get small projects started.
6. Support what is being done and the people doing it.
7. Extend contacts.
8. Encourage bigger groups and more groups.
9. Draw on adult education to train, support and encourage.
10. As groups develop reduce/withdraw direct support.
11. Look to new needs.
12. Keep up individual contacts—don't be swamped by committee.

The discussion then moved on to the ways in which neighbourhood workers and the project as a whole could influence statutory agencies.

The final day looked in detail at how the areas and neighbourhood workers had been selected. The group also considered how well the criteria for selecting neighbourhoods had been met. There was general satisfaction both with the procedures followed and meeting the selection criteria but there was a feeling that there needed to be more subsequent contact between the neighbourhoods and the project as a whole. The second theme for the day was CfND's work as a focus for community work training. Felicity and a committee member reviewed what had been achieved in internal training including the annual conferences; support to workers from other agencies; and help to individuals and groups in communities. They also looked at the lessons learned and considered what the future priorities should be. The final session for the day was on the dispersal of ideas—how well CfND had succeeded in demonstrating the value of the work it had been doing.

The report produced by ITS concluded that:

- CfND had generally developed in accordance with its aims but needed to develop more concrete objectives.
- The use of consensus had proved demanding and the area of group skills needed to be developed.
- CfND's approach to community development worked well.
- CfND's work in neighbourhoods could be strengthened by setting up local support groups.

- Agencies had been generally helpful and cooperative with CfND but if agencies were to be influenced then CfND as a whole needed to put more emphasis on this.
- The training and support to CfND staff had been very important in developing the effectiveness of the neighbour hood work.

ITS also noted that CfND was reaching the end of its development stage and in looking to the future it needed to keep certain key areas under review. These included the meaning of development in neighbourhoods; the relationship and influencing of statutory agencies; the role of CfND in carrying out research; the role of the central staff in direct community work and training; and the development of the committee as a working group.

In conjunction with the overall evaluation Lisa and a committee member carried out a specific evaluation of the work undertaken in the neighbourhoods. This detailed report provides the best picture of the work CfND had carried out in the selected neighbourhoods at that stage. It deals with the groups the workers were supporting, including new groups they had helped to set up, their relationships with statutory and voluntary agencies, their role in advice giving and the range of issues facing their areas.

1978 ONWARDS: NEW APPROACHES

Having completed the detailed evaluation and, by mid-1978, completed the recruitment of a worker in the sixth and final area, the project had reached the end of its first phase. At the beginning of 1978 Felicity moved away from Belfast and left CfND and towards the end of the same year Lisa also moved on. Although they were quickly replaced neither of their replacements had Quaker connections. The Quaker influence on the committee was still fairly strong, the trustees were still Quakers and the project was still housed in the Friends Institute but this year saw the lessening of the Quaker influence.

One of the significant events of 1978 was a change in the financial status of CfND. From its inception CfND had received its funding mainly from Quaker sources including meetings, legacies and trusts. However in 1978 for the first time CfND received some funding from the Belfast City Council. This followed detailed exploration of the potential sources of statutory funding given that

80

community development did not fit neatly into the remit of any particular statutory body at the time. The grant from the Council made up 20% of the overall expenditure in that year and from then on Belfast City Council supported CfND's work until the grant was withdrawn in 1992. The level of support increased significantly from the initial 20% to around 75-80% in the later years as it became increasingly difficult to raise funds for work which was no longer seen as new and innovative.

The difficulty for CfND was that, while Belfast City Council accepted the need for support, the other two Councils, i.e., Lisburn (Twinbrook) and Castlereagh (Cregagh), were less supportive. Castlereagh gave some limited support but Lisburn didn't offer any grant aid, despite a strong case being made to them. In 1980 it became clear that, without significant statutory support from Councils, the work outside Belfast could not continue and CfND had to withdraw from Cregagh in 1980 and Twinbrook in 1983. Work in Cregagh continued, however, as Castlereagh Council decided to employ its own neighbourhood workers. The work in Twinbrook was limited by the fact that Lilian was never able to secure an office base for her work and always had to work from home, a consequence of the lack of community facilities, one of the reasons the area was selected in the first place! CfND continued as a Belfast-based community development agency until 1992. Throughout this period it faced financial pressures. The 1980s were difficult times for any organisation relying on Council funding because, as well as the usual financial pressures, Councils had stopped working in the normal way because of disengagement of the Unionist councillors in the wake of the Anglo-Irish Agreement. In 1986 a letter was written to Tom King, Secretary of State for Northern Ireland, explaining what the organisation did and its history and making a case for direct Government funding. The letter started as follows:

'The Centre for Neighbourhood Development is one of a number of community organisations which have been affected by the stopping of grant-aid from Belfast City Council. As a result of this lack of finance CFND is likely to have to close within the next few weeks.'
Bass, Abbott and Graham (CfND 1986)

CfND survived this crisis but became aware of the risks to the organisation of the withdrawal of funding. It also became apparent that, while CfND's structure had served it well since the start, it did not have any legal basis as an organisation, so in 1986 it became a company limited by guarantee. The committee members became Company Directors and formal Annual General Meetings were held. Staff members could not be Directors and, because the organisation wanted to continue with the involvement of staff at committee meetings, the Directors devolved their day-to-day duties to a committee on which the staff were members. The Centre became more and more reliant on Belfast City Council funding. Voluntary sources covered the 25% balance including continued support from Quaker meetings and charitable trusts. John Moores Foundation, the Ireland Fund, War on Want and Oxfam were among the donors. Finance also came from some unusual sources such as the proceeds of a 1977 concert given by Steve Harley and Cockney Rebel and income from events like a fashion show in the Europa Hotel in 1988, organised by a fundraiser employed at that time.

In the late 1980s City Council funding was reduced and the organisation looked to other sources such as the Belfast Action Teams, a government regeneration initiative, which covered some of the costs of work in the New Lodge and Short Strand areas. In 1991, with the employment of the Council's own neighbourhood workers, Belfast City Council decided to end its funding. Despite a concerted campaign, CfND had to close and make the remaining workers redundant in 1992. The work did not come to a complete halt, particularly in Lower Oldpark where Betty Rice continued working for the local Community Association and in New Lodge, where Seamus McAloran kept working with the Ashton Centre project.

COMMUNITY ECONOMIC DEVELOPMENT

In the 1980s CfND's single biggest initiative was its work in the field of community economic development. The idea was to create employment within local communities with some element of community control over the projects created. The concern came from the recognition that one of the most serious problems in all the neighbourhoods was that of unemployment, both among adults and among young people. Male unemployment in each of the areas was at least 25% and in some cases much higher. Committee members were convinced that locally based and controlled employment initiatives would provide more sustainable and rewarding employment opportunities than could be provided by other means. This was very much a pioneering initiative at the time but its merits have been demonstrated in both the developed and developing world since then.

Discussions in 1980 and 1981, particularly at the Annual Conferences, led to the idea of taking on an additional member of staff in the Central Office as an Economic Development Worker liaising with the neighbourhood workers on job creation projects. Plans for a two-year pilot project were drawn up and discussed with potential funding agencies. In due course funding was obtained from the Northern Ireland Voluntary Trust* (NIVT) and LEDU, the Government's small business support agency and a worker, Stephen Rourke, was appointed in May 1983.

Stephen's first task was to analyse the issues and opportunities in each of the five neighbourhoods CfND was working in at the time. He then went on to develop initiatives in each of the areas through local groups. With his encouragement a range of youth training and Action for Community Employment (ACE) schemes were developed. One particularly ambitious project was to establish a small gardening cooperative in the Lower Oldpark area. While this scheme did a lot of good work, in the end the people involved felt that it was too complex to run their own business. In Stephen's first year an evaluation of the project showed that he had supported the creation of jobs for 57 people. The evaluation also confirmed the importance of the link between local community workers or community groups and an economic development specialist.

Stephen left the project during its second year and CfND then took time to re-evaluate the work and develop a revised approach. This involved linking with NIVT, the Northern Ireland Co-operative Development Agency and the Belfast Centre for the Unemployed to set up the Community Economic Development Initiative (CEDI). CEDI aimed to employ Economic Development Workers in several areas starting in Belfast. A formal agreement was signed between the agencies and a first worker appointed in 1987. Sharon O'Connor was initially based in CfND and worked particularly with Seamus McAloran in the New Lodge area. Her

* NIVT now Community Foundation for Northern Ireland (CFNI).

work centred around the Ashton Centre, a former warehouse which had been identified as a building or site for community use within the New Lodge area. The CEDI project did not expand beyond the initial worker but its work through Sharon was critical in getting the Ashton Centre up and running.

Sharon opened an office on the Antrim Road, where a job club was run to help New Lodge people find employment. After various feasibility studies examining how economic development and community activities could be accommodated, a new building was erected on the site with funds from Government and the International Fund for Ireland. Initially it housed a community-run supermarket, six shops, the Job Club, a training suite, a computer training room and eleven workshop units. The building was formally opened by Tom Foley, Speaker of the US House of Representatives, in 1991 and was owned and managed by a community based cooperative. While some elements of the original project, such as the supermarket, did not work out well, the building has been a major centre for the New Lodge community ever since.

REFLECTIONS

During its lifetime, CfND had made a significant contribution to community work in Belfast. It is hard to summarise the work carried out in the neighbourhoods over the life of the project but perhaps the best quick summary of the types of work carried out can be taken from a mid-1980s fundraising leaflet which broke the work down into four main areas as follows:

1. Youth

CFND provides creative outlets for youth through the provision of: Adventure Clubs, Unemployed Support Groups, ACE schemes, After School Groups, YTP Training Initiatives, Information Technology Training Course, target Recruitment Scheme, music bands, Arts and crafts, drama and discussion groups, summer schemes, sports clubs and cross community holiday projects.

2. Elderly

To deal with social isolation and combat the vulnerability which many pensioners feel CFND organises: Luncheon Clubs, Entertainment Groups, Oral History and Discussion Classes,

Plate 1 – Volunteers on first Irish Quaker Work Camps' Ballymurphy Playscheme, 1970.

Plate 2 – Irish Quaker Work Camps: Group of young people from Ballymurphy on a trip to Bangor, 1970.

*Plate 3 – Children playing at Ulster Quaker Service Committee's
Visitors' Centre, Maze Prison.*

Plate 4 – Mothers' Group at Quaker Cottage.

Plate 5 – Children playing at Quaker Cottage.

Plate 6 – Three views of Quaker Cottage: the original cottage; the purpose built building with view over Belfast; and the building in 2009.

Plate 7 – Ulster Quaker Service Committee Appeal leaflet 1983 illustrating types of work with photographs of Senior Citizens bus trip and caravan holiday.

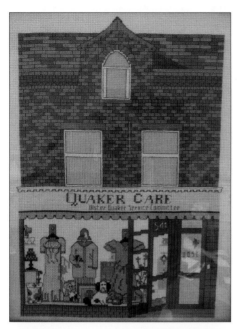

*Plate 8 – First Quaker Care
shop and Quaker Service office,
Lisburn Road, Belfast.*
(Needlepoint by kind permission
of Joan Ewing)

*Plate 9 – Opening of Quaker Care by Mo Mowlam, Secretary of State,
1998. Also showing from right: David Bass, Vincent Bent and the
unknown passer-by who Mo Mowlam picked out from onlookers
to do the actual opening!*

Plate 10 – Martie Rafferty receiving Butler Award from Princess Anne for work at Maze Prison.

Plate 11 – Ulster Quakers panel from Quaker Tapestry currently on display in Kendal, Cumbria, UK. (© Quaker Tapestry Scheme.) www.quaker-tapestry.co.uk. See Glossary for details.

Plate 12 – Quaker House Committee, 2006.

Plate 13 – Quaker House, 7 University Avenue, Belfast.

Plate 14 – Centre for Neighbourhood Development's first headquarters at Friends Institute, Frederick Street, Belfast.

Plate 15 – Cartoon from Centre for Neighbourhood Development Annual Report 1977, illustrating Community Education work.

Plate 16 – Cartoon from Centre for Neighbourhood Development Annual Report 1978.

Plate 17 – Lisa Huber (now Ann Le Mare), Centre for Neighbourhood Development's Development Officer, with residents in redevelopment area in Belfast.

Plate 18 – Quaker Peace Education Project Peer Mediation Group with certificates.

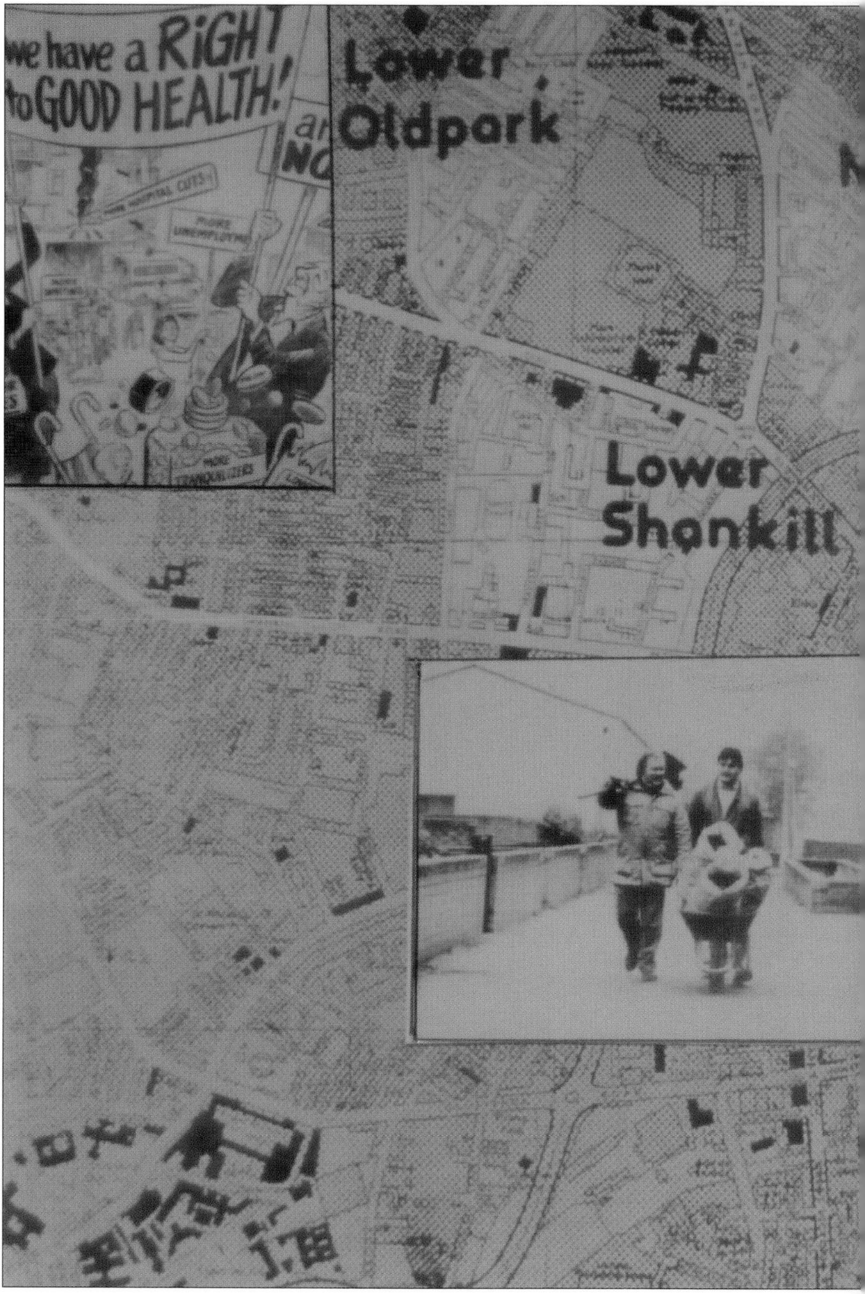
we have a RIGHT
to GOOD HEALTH!
Lower
Oldpark
Lower
Shankill

*Plate 19 –
Map from Centre for
Neighbourhood
Development Annual
Report 1988/9
showing four
neighbourhoods with
samples of projects in
each area; Short
Strand – St Matthews
Community Centre;
Lower Oldpark –
Health Project; Lower
Shankill –
environmental
workers; New Lodge –
Ashton Centre,
community economic
development project.*

Plate 20 – Quaker Peace Education Project Annual P7 Conference.

*Plate 21 – Quaker Peace Education Project: Rev. Nelson Onono-Oweng,
now Anglican Bishop of Gulu, Uganda with Jerry Tyrrell
during visit to project.*

Plate 22 – Quaker Peace Education Project Peer Mediation Training Group.

Plate 23 – Quaker Peace Education Project Annual P7 Conference.

*Plate 24 – Quaker Peace Education Project Peer Mediation Group visit
to meet President Mary Robinson.*

Leisure Trips, Decorating and grass cutting service, Social evenings.

3. Women
CFND has identified a clear need for specific work with women to encourage personal development and integration into the community. The range of activities includes: Women and Health Classes, Assertion Training, Education Initiatives, Second Chance to Learn, Creative Writing, Arts and Crafts, Traditional and Non-traditional skills, Mother and Toddlers Groups, Holiday schemes, Crèches, Social Events.

4. Services to the Unemployed
Both the Lower Shankill and Lower Oldpark operate success-ful ACE schemes which provide temporary employment for 40 people. CFND operates 'clubs', the focus of which is to help young people in their search for employment.

One aspect of work which was not often highlighted was that of community relations. This was because it was always seen as a by-product of the main work since the emphasis was always on the development of communities within specific neighbourhoods. This was later referred to as 'Single Identity Work' (Hughes & Donnelly 1997). However, there were numerous examples of training programmes, joint visits and other events which brought together people from communities on both sides of the political divide at a time when it was not easy to do so.

During the 15 years of CfND, there was only one change of personnel at neighbourhood level, in contrast to central staff who changed over the years both in terms of personnel and responsi-bilities. The central roles identified at the beginning were appro-priate for a new and expanding organisation but they needed to change to reflect the changed circumstances. The post of Co-ordi-nator became a focal point for the organisation. A second central office role came under various titles such as Field Support Worker and was always engaged in training initiatives, research and project evaluation. The staff also became involved in certain elements of work in the neighbourhoods, for example a Health Project devel-oped and piloted in the Lower Oldpark area in 1985. This project started with a Public Meeting to identify health issues facing people in the area. These included problems of fumes from new solid fuel fires, the lack of safe play facilities for children, poor access to GPs, nowhere for teenagers to meet and the need for a pedestrian crossing on a dangerous road. The meeting resulted in the setting up of a local health group which focussed on these issues.

The one neighbourhood where there was a change in personnel was in Short Strand. Danny Taggart died suddenly on his way to a CfND committee meeting in May 1988. Danny had made an extraordinary contribution to the Short Strand community during his time in CfND and this is reflected in an article in the 1988/9 CfND Annual Report. The following extracts indicate not only Danny's particular contribution, but also show the sort of contribution CfND made in the four areas.

> *'Virtually every improvement in the quality of life in the area seemed to have Danny's hand in it at some stage.... [He] was a leading figure in the Tenants Association ... was very much involved in the negotiations to secure the move [of the Sirocco factory] ... was involved in the establishment of the MacAirt Community Centre ... served on the management committee of the local Primary Schools ... was one of the leading figures in setting up the St. Matthews Housing Association ... one of the first community-based Housing Associations in Northern Ireland.*

> *'He played significant roles in a wide variety of Belfast-wide organisations ... he was very much involved in the Association of Local Advice Centres ... from this came his involvement in the setting up and management of the Belfast Law Centre.... Another major involvement was in the District Health Committee.*

> *'Danny always worked very carefully taking time to listen and take into account what other people said'.*

(CfND Annual Report 88/9 pgs. 27-8)

In 1984/5 CfND celebrated its tenth anniversary in various ways, including a party with a cake! It held a Three-Day Community Work Symposium in December in the Ulster People's College. This was attended by over 100 people interested in community work and included sessions on advice and advocacy, the impact of the Troubles on social policy and community development, statutory/voluntary cooperation and community self help. Addresses were given by various leading community activists. The 1983/4 Annual Report was a 10-year report including a review of 'Tendencies in Community Work' by Hugh Frazer of Northern

Ireland Voluntary Trust and a review of 10 years of CfND. In his article Hugh Frazer commented on how

'organisations like CfND have kept alive some of the beliefs, from the early 1970s, such as the need for fundamental social change, the importance of personal development, the need for a more centralised society and the encouragement of self-help and community involvement'.

(CfND Annual Report 83/4)

Hugh concluded by 'congratulating CfND on its ten years of achievement and above all for helping to keep alive the belief that community work is more about people than about buildings' (ibid).

CfND had many successes and many of its original aims were achieved but the fact that it closed in the early 1990s suggests that perhaps it did not adapt to changes successfully and may even have been constrained by some of the Quaker influences. Some of the early decisions taken affected the future workings of the organisation. The use of consensus was an obvious measure given the Quaker style of running meetings but it did mean that decisions often took a long time to take and in some cases may simply have been avoided. Similarly the idea of involving staff in all the decisions taken often posed difficulties.

One of the main tensions that existed in CfND was the tension between the three core elements of the project – the central office staff, the neighbourhood workers and the voluntary committee members. This was linked to the challenge facing the neighbourhood workers. Who were their masters? Did they work for a central office manager, the committee or their own communities? CfND was never able to involve community representatives fully in the organisation (with one notable exception). This may have been at least partly because the neighbourhood workers did not feel comfortable with the idea of having someone they worked closely with in the neighbourhood on the management committee.

CONCLUSIONS

In a letter expressing his regret that CfND was closing down, Stephen Pittam of Joseph Rowntree Charitable Trust wrote as follows:

'I remember the excitement that was around when the project was first set up. It was able to carry forward some of the hope that had been generated by the Community Development Programme of the former Community Relations Commission. The idea of employing local people as community workers and offering training and support from the Centre was well founded. The project has been well served by the commitment offered by both its staff members and members of its Management Committee. CFND has a lot to celebrate.'

Joseph Rowntree Charitable Trust 1992

It is worth considering what the project achieved and what was the Quaker input to its outcomes. There is no doubt that Quakers were well placed to start the project in 1974. Respected on both sides of the community they were able to work at grass roots level in communities effectively at war with each other. There were statutory bodies working throughout Northern Ireland right through the Troubles but they had problems in getting into the heart of individual communities. There were also voluntary bodies providing services in specific neighbourhoods across the political divide. Examples of these were Save the Children Fund who ran play-groups and the Northern Ireland Adventure Playground Association. These organisations were successful and courageous in providing particular services in local communities, often in the face of street violence during the early phase of the Troubles. But the kind of work CfND carried out, with its emphasis on the involvement and development of communities and of networking across Belfast, was all too rare.

CfND also had the benefit of having two Friends who were experienced and respected Community Workers in the NICRC. Lisa and Felicity were able to bring their expertise to the new organisation and guide it over its early years. They were also able to bring on board a sound mixture of Friends and people from community work, social policy and reconciliation fields to run the organisation. Quakers influenced the ethics and methodology of the organisation in many ways – even down to the importance of keeping good records. (This chapter is based on a selection of documents which fill five large boxes and record all the main decisions, events and discussions!) It is difficult to identify clearly the extent of the Quaker influence on CfND's organisation but it can be seen in all the ideas below:

- Equal pay for workers;
- Staff involvement on the management committee;
- Involvement of neighbourhood representatives on the committee;
- The use of consensus;
- The emphasis on training, further education and support particularly for those without academic qualifications;
- The support for informal community relations work alongside community development; and
- A readiness to hand over work to other agencies after a pilot phase.

The original aims listed earlier in this chapter were largely achieved. The influence the project had in all the neighbourhoods it worked in was enormous, both in terms of the physical development of the areas, the facilities introduced to the areas, the services run and, most importantly, the development of the community workers and leaders. It shone a light in days of despair for many local communities. In addition it pioneered many new developments in community work and influenced the direction community development took in Belfast. Stephen Pittam was right. There was a lot to celebrate. Quakers were able to mobilise the resources to start this work and prove its worth. In fact, it is doubtful if it would have started in 1975 without their commitment, personnel and funding, but it was right that the work evolved and was taken up by Councils and others in the community development field. That was the legacy for Northern Ireland, for reconciliation and for community development.

References

Cadbury, P. S. (1974) 'Friends Ambulance Unit' Davies, A. Tegla cited in **Official and Unofficial Quaker Service.**

Centre for Neighbourhood Development (CfND) (14 October 1974) **Minutes,** Steering Committee Meeting.

CfND (November 1974) **Community Work Policy.**

CfND (1983/1984) **Annual Report.**

CfND (11 April 1986) **Letter to Tom King, Secretary of State for Northern Ireland.**, from F. Bass (Convenor), M. Abbott (Secretary) and C. Graham (Treasurer).

CfND (1988/1989) **Annual Report.** Pages 27-28.

CfND (1991) Fund Raising Leaflet.

Huber, L. & McCartney, F. (July 1974) **Discussion paper.**

Huber, L. & McCartney, F. (1980) 'An Experience in Supporting Neighbourhood Work' in Henderson, Jones & Thomas (eds.) **The Boundaries of Change in Community Work** London: George Allen & Unwin.

Hughes, J. & Donnelly, C. (1997) **Single Identity Community Relations in Northern Ireland:** School of Public Policy, Economics & Law University of Ulster at Jordanstown (UUJ).

Joseph Rowntree Charitable Trust (25 March 1992) **Letter from Stephen Pittam,** Assistant Trust Secretary, to CfND.

McKay, S. (2000) **Northern Protestants, An Unsettled People.** Belfast: Blackstaff Press.

Chapter 5

QUAKER HOUSE BELFAST

Anne Bennett

A HISTORY OF THE WORK OF QUAKER HOUSE
1982-2007

'I pin my hopes to quiet processes and small circles, in which vital and transforming events take place'.
Rufus Jones 1937

INTRODUCTION

THIS CHAPTER covers the work of a conciliation project in Belfast from 1982-2007. It follows the development chronologically through interviews with successive staff (called the Representatives) showing how the work was responsive to political and community events, and how each phase drew on relationships built previously as well as the skills and experience of each appointee. A final section examines the structures set up to support the Belfast project, involving Quaker organisations in London and Dublin as well as local Friends.

The model of a Quaker House has been used successfully in various parts of the world.* It follows a pattern of establishing a house as an informal meeting place in a safe, neutral location, with resident staff available to meet with people who might be able to make a difference in a conflict or post conflict situation. The emphasis is on informality and meetings are often held over a shared meal enabling the Representatives to listen to the views

---

* See Chapter 1 section on Quaker Centres, p.8. 91

of different sides in a conflict and helping them to make wider contacts (Yarrow 1978).

Quaker House Belfast grew out of an existing programme of Resident Friends with experience of conflict situations working as volunteers and living in accommodation at Frederick Street Meeting House in North Belfast over the period 1972-1977 (see Chapter 2). The programme was organised by Quakers in Britain and supported by Quakers in Ireland, both North and South. The Resident Friends met with politicians, community and church leaders, linked with other peace organisations and brought together individuals who wished to meet in a safe environment. The work was confidential, based on respect and the recognition that Quakers were committed to non-violence. It was a phase of useful work for making contacts that laid the foundation for Quaker House work in the future. The initial project was supported by an Ireland Watching Committee made up of knowledgeable Quakers in Ireland and Britain.

Volunteers with this project were able to give varying periods of service but it became apparent that there was a need for a more consistent approach, so after further consultations, Quaker House Belfast was established in 1982. Its purpose was 'to further the work of reconciliation and of befriending all parties in Northern Ireland'. It was felt important that Quakers

> *'should not advocate any particular overall solution; in fact it is our view that it could be harmful if Quakers were regarded as advocates of any particular view, rather than principles based on their religious beliefs such as reconciliation and the rejection of violent means to achieve any ends'.*

QPS 1984

The main areas of work were to be: bringing together people who would not otherwise meet; recognizing and valuing diversity; creating a neutral and safe place so that people could be more open in their discussions; helping people to work on sensitive issues relevant to reconciliation; reflecting the views of Friends and increasing their awareness.

Quaker Peace and Service, London (QPS)* formed the Northern Ireland Committee consisting of six Friends from Ireland

---

* QPS was a shared department of both Britain and Ireland YM at that time.

Yearly Meeting, three from the North and three from the South with six from Britain. A further three could be appointed to achieve inclusion and equality. The Northern Ireland Committee was to oversee the work of Quaker House Belfast and maintain links with decision makers in London and Dublin. In 1982 QPS purchased 7, University Avenue, situated in a quiet area accessible to all and near Queen's University. The first Representatives, William and Joan Sinton, were appointed in July 1982.

WILLIAM (BILLY) AND JOAN SINTON*
July 1982 - June 1984

Billy and Joan were Quakers from Northern Ireland and had been involved with the previous project since its inception. Billy had, in addition to his involvement with his farm and a farm products company, been on the Board of Visitors at the Maze Prison and Chair of the Board of Visitors for Special Category Prisoners at the time of the Hunger Strike. Joan had been involved with the Visitors Centre at The Maze and other social work. They were appointed in July and took up residence at Quaker House in September 1982. Their period of service came to an end in June 1984 as a result of Billy's ill health.

Northern Ireland 1982-1984.

The Hunger Strike by Republican prisoners in Maze/Long Kesh Prison had come to an end in October 1981 but there were many issues emerging from this stressful period. The IRA and the INLA were active in Northern Ireland and Britain. In 1983 the New Ireland Forum was established. It was a period of uncertainty and mistrust on all sides.

AREAS OF WORK

Much of the Sintons' early work involved establishing Quaker House and ensuring that its purpose was understood. It was important to communicate the ethos of the work and to build trust with people of varying views, ensuring that there were firm foundations to carry the work forward after they left. Billy and Joan made relationships with a number of individuals and groups including

---

* Based on an interview with Joan Sinton on 30.5.08. Billy Sinton died in 1985 and Joan in 2009.

politicians, paramilitary groups, prisoners, peace groups, church representatives and cross community groups. This was often slow and they were ready to visit, offer friendship and a neutral space, listening without judging and accepting that they could be rejected by some factions. They established links with possible allies and built on Quakers' known reputation for work in the prisons. They began by visiting people, introducing themselves and indicating their willingness to listen, made connections and offers of hospitality. After a first round of visits they waited for openings to emerge and gradually people contacted them and areas of work emerged. Each piece of work took a different form, being shaped by the needs and opportunities as presented.

Politicians and Paramilitaries

Politicians and members of paramilitary organisations were willing to come to Quaker House for a meal and to discuss their views, hopes and fears with Quakers and invited guests. During their tenure the Sintons concentrated on work with politicians from within the UK. Links with politicians from the Irish Republic were to come later. A similar pattern of meeting and listening was established with paramilitary organisations, at a time when they were not widely politically acceptable.

As relationships evolved, individual politicians, paramilitary and community leaders came regularly to Quaker House to talk about the situation, clarify their thinking and explore the views of others. Although the different groups did not meet face to face, they knew that Billy and Joan were meeting and listening to other individuals and groups and that Quaker House was a place where they would be welcomed and heard. Given the nature of the political situation, this was part of a slow process to establish contact across the full breadth of opinion and it set the agenda for future work. The process also led Quaker House to make a submission to the New Ireland Forum in 1983 urging the Forum 'to encourage every opportunity for listening, understanding and respecting one another without any attempt at coercion to another point of view' (QHB Statement 1983).

Community and Peace Work

The Representatives developed and maintained links with a range of community groups. Some came to Quaker House as established groups while others were in the process of trying to form and needed a neutral space to hold their initial meetings. They ranged from strong loyalist and republican working class groups to middle class groups such as a cross community group of solicitors. Although these groups came from different backgrounds, the Representatives found it interesting that they were all working on similar issues.

Joan was involved with individuals from houses close to the Peace Line in Belfast who were at the receiving end of missiles thrown from across the wall. She walked along both sides of the Peace Line knocking on doors, and talking to people about their situation. After some time, she was able to bring together women from the two communities for a meeting at Quaker House, out of which grew a more formal group that the Sintons and their successors continued to support. Other cross community work included support for the newly opened Lagan College, the first Integrated School* in Northern Ireland.

Quaker House had a specific concern about the use of plastic bullets in crowd control and used its contacts to meet with senior staff within the Royal Ulster Constabulary (RUC)** and the Northern Ireland Office to convey public concern about their use and misuse within the confines of parades and riots. The Sintons built close working links with a number of Peace and church groups, listening, supporting and using Quaker House as a meeting place for those with a commitment to sustainable peace in Northern Ireland to get together.

Some of their work involved engaging with Irish and British Quakers, informing them about ongoing developments and including them in the work at Quaker House. There were numerous Quaker and non-Quaker visitors from North America. Some of these visitors were well informed but others had little understanding of the complexities of the political situation and the need for quiet listening. The Representatives spent many hours explaining the political situation and arranging for visitors to meet local people.

---

* An Integrated School is one where Protestant and Catholic children are educated together.
** Later the RUC was disbanded and the Police Service of Northern Ireland (PSNI) set up.

Prisoners

Billy's previous involvement on the Board of Visitors at The Maze Prison and his involvement with the Committee for the Administration of Justice* (CAJ) enabled a continuation of the concern for the work in the prisons. The experiences of the Life Sentence Prisoners known as 'Lifers' and the anxieties in the aftermath of the Hunger Strikes brought contact with the Northern Ireland Office and the prisoners and their families. Relatives of Northern Irish prisoners held in British prisons found it difficult to visit and the Sintons were able to involve British Quakers in supporting them when they travelled to England, a piece of work that continued after they left.

REFLECTIONS

The work of establishing Quaker House, building up its credibility and engaging with a cross section of society in Northern Ireland at this time was stressful, and demanding of both Billy and Joan. Keeping contacts alive, being prepared for the physical demands of running the house, helping to set up meetings that might or might not come to anything took their toll. A report on the work of Quaker House towards the end of Billy and Joan's tenure said,

'The Representatives have listened to and counselled with many shades of opinion and leadership in Ireland including those who have moderate and those who have paramilitary behaviour. Contacts have been furthered with the churches, the Northern Ireland Office, key people within the political parties, community leaders and with informal and professional groups concerned with finding the way forward out of the present troubles. From time to time the Representatives have urged men of violence to cease from taking vengeance over a particular murder and to give up the gun for the ballot box'.

NIC Report 1984

The emphasis during this phase was to establish contacts and lay the foundation for future work. Billy and Joan had an open approach to both established politicians and people from communities who were experiencing the worst effects of the conflict. Many people wanted to talk about the problems and possible solutions

---

* CAJ: A voluntary sector human rights organisation in Northern Ireland.

and there were anxieties about the future of Northern Ireland. Quaker House provided opportunities for some of those people to talk about their ideas and be listened to and to hear the strongly held views of others.

Sadly, Billy Sinton was admitted to hospital in May 1984 and was unable to return to Quaker House. Joan continued on her own until mid-June by which time the next Representatives had been appointed.

JOHN AND EDITH WIGZELL*
May 1984 – May 1987
John and Edith were English Friends and Edith had a long-standing connection with Northern Ireland. John had served with the Probation Service and the Home Office Inspectorate and Edith as a Health Visitor. On retirement they applied for and were appointed as the second Representatives at Quaker House. They were able to engage in a formal handover of the work and enjoyed their work in Belfast.

Northern Ireland 1984-1987

This was a period of suspicion, lack of dialogue and gestures by many of the principal groups to try to impose their authority. The IRA was active within Northern Ireland and in England, including the bombing in October 1984 of the Grand Hotel in Brighton during the Conservative Party Conference. In 1985 Margaret Thatcher and Irish Taoiseach** Garrett FitzGerald signed the Anglo-Irish Agreement and a month later all 15 Unionist MPs at Westminster resigned in protest. Six months later the Northern Ireland Assembly, which had been set up in 1982 in an attempt to restore devolution to Northern Ireland, was officially dissolved and the Province was governed by direct rule from Westminster.

AREAS OF WORK

John and Edith recognised the need to develop the work started by their predecessors and respond to new opportunities

---

* Based on an interview with Edith Wigzell on 19.3.08. John Wigzell died in 2005.
** Irish Prime Minister.

97

as they arose. They developed links with emerging political figures and established contact with politicians and decision-shapers in the Republic of Ireland. John's probation background would enable him to build on work with the prisons and prisoners' families and to strengthen links with Lifers. They looked for opportunities to extend the work through reading local newspapers, watching TV and by attending meetings where the political situation was discussed.

Politicians, Paramilitaries and Prisons

Some local politicians felt sufficiently comfortable with Quaker House that they responded to the Representatives' offer of space for meetings that would take place at the House but without John and Edith attending. These included confidential meetings between members of the SDLP and the Official Unionist parties.

The Wigzells continued the practice of inviting local and Westminster politicians to Quaker House to encourage dialogue. This was especially important after the return to direct rule from Westminster when there was no Assembly in Belfast. Senior members of all the Northern Ireland political parties were invited to Quaker House and many took up the invitation. Some became regular visitors and seemed to value the opportunities provided. Links with politicians from the South included talking with Garrett FitzGerald about options for peace and meeting with Mary Robinson, a respected Human Rights lawyer, before she became President of Ireland and a visit to the Irish Embassy in London. These meetings with politicians and Irish civil servants were often arranged and attended with Friends from Ireland or Britain. The Representatives were enabled by Quaker Peace and Service, London (QPS) to meet a number of Westminster MPs with responsibility for Northern Ireland. Participants came from all parties and they shared a common interest in exploring Northern Ireland issues in more detail. This was an area of work to be developed by Quaker House in the future. While working with local politicians, they also developed links with a succession of Secretaries of State for Northern Ireland and senior members of the Northern Ireland Office (NIO), many of whom came to Quaker House to talk and to listen.

Links were maintained with paramilitary leaders and their wider membership who were willing to participate in meetings, enabling the sharing of ideas even though the groups might not meet face to face. It was a step towards direct exchange in the future.

Working with the Ulster Quaker Service Committee (UQSC) staff at the Maze Prison,* John was able to build on previous prison work, focussing on a number of issues including the strip searching of women visitors, a practice which aroused considerable anger but seemed not to have a complaints process. The Representatives talked with civil servants in the Northern Ireland Office and with the Secretary of State for Northern Ireland, conveying the anger generated by such inhumane procedures. In time this practice was changed. Their concern about prisoner conditions at the Maze and Maghaberry Prisons and their support for the Quaker work at the Visitors' Centres resulted in some prisoners remaining in contact with Quaker House on leaving prison, when some of them would be politicians or community leaders.

Community Groups, Churches and Peace

Edith and John continued the contacts with community groups and people living on or near the Peace Line in West Belfast, encouraging community employment opportunities and some cross community contact activities including participation in events arranged by the Corrymeela Community. New opportunities included involvement with setting up the Family Mediation Organization at Bryson House and a venture with a group of Catholic and Protestant couples working together on a Marriage Enrichment Course. The Wigzells had previously served as counsellors with RELATE** and were pleased that members of the course continued to work together after they had left. They supported Integrated Schools and met with staff and pupils of Lagan College and the newly founded Hazelwood College and organised meetings for local Friends to learn more about integrated education.

The Representatives developed connections with church leaders and had discussions with a Catholic bishop about Integrated Schools, to which he was strongly opposed. They also had the opportunity to attend an all-Ireland meeting of church leaders. These connections led to opportunities for discussions with

---

* Previously Long Kesh.
** A relationship counselling organisation.

members and clergy from other denominations, who were working on some of the same issues as Quaker House but in different settings. They were also able to support local peace groups, some of which met at Quaker House, and a local initiative to hold a 'tea party' on Garvaghy Road, in Portadown, to help diffuse tensions during the Drumcree Orange Parades (see Chapter 2). They were careful to support the work of local people in this sort of situation without having an organizing role.

REFLECTIONS

This phase was characterized by deep suspicion of cross community contact, the marginalisation of paramilitary groups and the negative reaction of Unionists to the Anglo-Irish Agreement. In this context, Quaker House was able to provide opportunities for contact and was seen as making a positive contribution to the process of talking and listening. The Representatives recognised that such work is part of a long process and at times it felt like pushing a large rock up a hill! They regarded themselves as facilitators, not mediators and hoped that in offering a safe space for meetings whether they attended themselves or not, they were assisting the overall process

Unfortunately, John Wigzell suffered a heart attack from which he made a full recovery but it curtailed their work in the last few months. They completed their service as planned in May 1987.

STEVE AND SUE WILLIAMS*
July 1987 - September 1991
Sue and Steve were Friends from the USA with considerable experience of developing confidence-building programmes in areas of conflict such as Haiti and East Africa. They were in Northern Ireland on a speaking tour about their recent work in Uganda when Quaker House advertised for new Representatives.

Northern Ireland 1987-1991

There was little contact between the political groupings and in many cases elected representatives from different parties did not

---

* Based on an interview with Sue Williams on 27.7.08. Steve Williams had died in 2007.

speak to each other during this period. Repercussions after the signing of the Anglo-Irish Agreement led to the Unionists being the most marginalised group and they sensed that Governments could reach agreements without engaging them in the process. There was ongoing killing of individuals by paramilitary groups on both sides, the IRA conducted high profile attacks including the Remembrance Sunday bomb at Enniskillen, the SAS killed three members of the IRA in Gibraltar and then three mourners at their funeral were killed by Michael Stone of UVF, all compounding a sense of mistrust and withdrawal into 'safe areas'.

AREAS OF WORK

Much of the community work begun by previous Representatives had been devolved or moved on, so Steve and Sue felt that they should concentrate on developing stronger links with the paramilitary groups and with Unionists, now marginalised by their opposition to the Anglo-Irish Agreement. They also identified a need to strengthen relationships with Irish political parties and senior civil servants in Dublin. They identified the purpose of their work as to concentrate on the 'broken circle of communication' between the various interests.

Political work and Paramilitary Groups

Steve and Sue met with representatives from the paramilitary groups, listening and reflecting with them on their views, on the views of other groups and on their reactions to current events. Existing contact with Lifers was extended, working with Martie Rafferty of UQSC who knew this group through her prison work (Chapter 3). Prisoners had a key role in developing strategy for their respective paramilitary organisations, as they had time and access to information through the Prison library and contact was maintained by Quaker House after their release. At this time Westminster MPs from Northern Ireland unionist and nationalist parties did not publicly acknowledge each other. Opposing politicians and paramilitaries came to Quaker House, first meeting with the Representatives, and then, when they were ready, with each other. Steve and Sue used a shuttle mediation approach, carrying messages and providing information about the stance of other parties. They decided in advance of meetings which one would take responsibility for its content. They did not take notes during the meeting but one was in charge of talking and the other taking mental notes of dialogue, body language, points to follow up, etc. For example, during three years of their time at Quaker House Sue and Steve participated in unofficial shuttle mediation between Unionists and politicians in Dublin. They were seen as a vehicle to reach out to others. It was not primarily about personal relationships but more about understanding the 'other' through the Representatives. They were trusted to relay messages confidentially, but it was a reactive, enabling role providing an insight into the thinking of those with whom they were working. It was in an environment where many were more worried about the actions of those on their own side and therefore needed to be sure how a new idea would be received by the other side before they would risk the disapproval of their own party. They established contacts with the Northern Ireland spokespersons in parties in the South and newly appointed ministers in departments that had links with the North, e.g., agriculture, who had to make contacts quickly in the North to learn about common issues. They undertook similar contacts with members of the Westminster Parliament.

Time was spent attending Belfast City Council and later other local councils, including the Dungannon and South Tyrone District Council which had an experimental committee to deal with contentious issues. This enabled them to be dealt with out of the public eye, where councillors might feel obliged to take a hard line position. During their time at Quaker House Steve and Sue arranged for small groups of Quakers to meet with politicians. Some Dublin politicians, for example, wanted to learn about programmes in the North. Politicians expected groups to lobby them but were surprised that individual Quakers did not share a political view and frequently disagreed with each other! This part of the programme enabled Quakers from the North and South to participate and share views with each other and with decision makers and shapers in Dublin.

Community Groups and Peace

In addition to the work described above, the Representatives engaged with other organisations involved in the community, especially those attempting to draw politicians' attention to issues such as health and education which were not on the political agenda. Sue was also involved with the setting up of the Northern Ireland Mediation Network.* Contacts with Dublin led to their connections with the Peace Train (organised by some Dublin politicians and Trades Union leaders), an attempt to draw attention to the unacceptability of regular bombs on the Belfast to Dublin railway line. Other Ulster Quaker Peace Committee members were involved in this campaign.

REFLECTIONS

Reflecting on the Anglo-Irish Agreement, Sue felt that although it had been the result of an exclusive process, and bitterly resented by Unionists at the time, it does not appear so now. It seems clear that it created structural changes, acknowledged a role for both governments and made it easier to consider shared sovereignty and changes to the Irish Constitution. It was one piece of the whole and on reflection contributed to addressing major needs which eventually would lead to a solution. There was also a series of surveys published in the newspapers indicating that there was no single, simple response to basic issues but complex responses. One such poll in the Irish Times looked at views in the South on a united Ireland to which the response was that it was desirable but not if the process was going to cost too much money. These positive contributions were often undermined by the tendency of politicians and community leaders to reject anything that did not meet their narrowly defined needs. The use of hypothetical questions in the media frequently resulted in a closing of options before they had an opportunity to be exposed to genuine debate.

The Williamses felt that their time at Quaker House was a contribution to a pattern of work that was very effective in engaging with the 'broken circle of communication'. Peace is a slow process and all of the actors, including civil society and government, have different roles and all contribute to the whole and finally reach a point where people can see something better than what they had.

Steve and Sue completed their period of service at Quaker House and left to work for Quakers in East Africa.

---

* Later known as Mediation Northern Ireland.

ALAN AND JANET QUILLEY*
February 1992 – July 1999
Alan and Janet were appointed as the Representatives at Quaker House in 1993. They were English Friends. Janet had a career in teaching and Alan in teaching and employment with an Examinations Board.

Northern Ireland 1993-1999

It was a time of uncertainty with disruption, a persistent round of killings and regular high profile bomb attacks in Northern Ireland and Britain, including the killing of 10 people by a bomb in a crowded fish shop on the Shankill Road and gun attacks on bars in Greysteel and Loughisland. In 1994 the IRA, followed by the Loyalist Military Command, announced ceasefires which the former ended 18 months later due to a lack of progress with the peace process. Politically there seemed to be little progress but the appointment by US President Clinton of Senator George Mitchell as a 'peace envoy', a Labour Government with Tony Blair as Prime Minister and the appointment of Dr. Marjorie 'Mo' Mowlam as Secretary of State for Northern Ireland contributed to the process which resulted in Sinn Fein and Unionists engaging in discussions leading to the Good Friday Agreement in April 1998.

AREAS OF WORK

There had been a gap of 17 months between the two sets of Representatives. During this period local Friends took care of Quaker House but there was no active programme. Alan and Janet spent some time educating themselves about the situation and establishing connections with decision makers, unsure as to which would lead to future work. Gradually they developed a programme of activities which included focussing on the tensions on the Ormeau Road, North/South links, Westminster MPs and connections within the community and church leaders. They also maintained links with Quakers in the North and South of Ireland trying to explain what was happening at Quaker House and raising awareness among Quakers in Britain by speaking to many local Meetings about their work.

* Based on an interview with Alan and Janet Quilley on 22.4.08.

Parades

There was a history of violence for several years when the Orangemen had traditionally marched down the Ormeau Road where their presence was resented by the mainly nationalist residents of Lower Ormeau Road close to Quaker House. Janet and Alan had developed links with members of the local Orange Lodge and with community leaders from Lower Ormeau who were both concerned about the violence and ways of ending it and approached Quaker House. This led to meetings with the different groups separately and later with their representatives meeting at Quaker House. In the summer of 1995 these were taking place nearly every day as they worked on a formula that respected the needs of both communities and minimized the risk of violence during parades. Once the Parades Commission was established in 1998, the Representatives continued their relationships with the community leaders and during parades would monitor behaviour, noting unacceptable behaviour and feeding in comments as appropriate. They maintained a non-partisan stance, difficult at times when being ready to listen and talk to the Orangemen, the nationalist community and the police.

Politicians

Early in their time at Quaker House Janet and Alan were able to build on relationships with Southern politicians and develop new relationships with emerging Loyalist party leaders, especially David Ervine and Billy Hutchinson of the Progressive Unionist Party (PUP). From these connections they were able to work with the Northern Ireland Mediation Network to organise two weekend meetings at Corrymeela, enabling Loyalist/Unionist and Southern groups to meet, in some cases for the first time. There was a hope that the members of loyalist paramilitary groups would reduce the level of violence if their leaders could show that they were being taken seriously by more established politicians. The participants at these gatherings remained in contact with Quaker House and provided links for formal and informal work in the future.

At the time of Alan and Janet's appointment the UK had a long standing Conservative Government but the indications were that at a future election they would be replaced by the Labour Party whose members' views on Northern Ireland included 'troops out'.

As a starting point, the Quilleys used Quaker connections with MPs at Westminster, especially within the Labour Party and their links with local politicians and church leaders to set up a programme to expose MPs and future members of the Northern Ireland Office to the situation in Northern Ireland. They identified MPs with an interest in Northern Ireland and sent out personal invitations hoping to have 6-8 MPs for each programme. They organised eight such gatherings for Labour MPs, one which involved Conservative MPs and one at the request of Mo Mowlam. Each involved 36 hours of meetings with politicians, church leaders and community workers. Local political parties sent senior members to talk with the MPs and the experience gave the participants an insight into the complexity of life in Northern Ireland.

The contact with Labour MPs and shadow Northern Ireland Secretary Mo Mowlam while in opposition provided a useful connection with the Government when it came to power. It also brought opportunities for Quaker House to engage a wider group in discussions about the Good Friday Agreement. Commentators, academics, prisoners and others with concerns about prison issues were some of those brought along as speakers. While the seminars for MPs were time consuming, the availability and flexibility of Quaker House was especially useful during this period. Politicians had a sense that they were coming to a meal in a home and not to an official meeting.

Community and Prison Work

Janet's involvement with Women in Faith grew out of an early meeting with Jean Mayhew, the wife of the Secretary of State for Northern Ireland, who expressed a wish to meet with local women. Janet arranged for her to meet with 10-12 women for tea at Quaker House. Jean Mayhew then organised a meeting of 120 women at Hillsborough discussing non-threatening issues out of which grew a small ecumenical group which met regularly to discuss some of the more uncomfortable issues in a relaxed setting.

Quaker House continued its association with Mediation Northern Ireland, with Alan acting as its Treasurer. Janet was secretary of the Faith and Politics group which had an ecumenical church membership from both the North and South and addressed some of the same issues as Quaker House in small, invited groups.

A number of Peace Groups including the Ulster Quaker Peace Committee and INNATE* met at Quaker House. The Representatives were involved with both groups and supported their activities including the preparation and publication of a booklet by INNATE entitled 'The South African experience – lessons for Northern Ireland'.

The Quaker House Penal Affairs Group, a development from the Lifers group, continued to meet, working on issues relating to the prisons and prisoners. The Representatives became members of this group and built on links with the prisons and with the Northern Ireland Office which led to useful contacts for other parts of their programme.

REFLECTIONS

The Quilleys were the longest serving Representatives and their time at Quaker House coincided with a time of unrest but there were also opportunities for movement that came as a result of the Good Friday Agreement. Parades became a major issue in Northern Ireland during this period and their work in Ormeau Road was significant in making contacts between opposing factions, with wider political interests and with the police. The role changed when the Government set up the Parades Commission, as it then dealt with official negotiations and agreements for each parade, but Quaker House still had a role in supporting the groupings they knew and remaining open to future contact. They continued the practice of building on previous work, using Quaker House as a setting for off the record meetings where politicians and community representatives had the opportunity to speak and be heard. It was a stimulating and enjoyable experience for Alan and Janet but they felt that they left at the right time. There would inevitably be political changes following the Agreement. There would be more direct contact between all the main players in the Northern Ireland scene and less need for the Quaker House style of work.

There was a five month gap between the departure of Alan and Janet and the appointment of their successor.

---

* Irish Network for Nonviolent Action, Training and Education. 107

> # MARK CHAPMAN*
> January 2000 - January 2004
> Mark was a local Quaker with experience of work with Peace Brigades International in Sri Lanka and with the Gulf Peace Team before being appointed to Quaker House. Although he was accompanied by his family, Mark was the first Representative at Quaker House to work as a single Representative.

Northern Ireland 2000-2004

The Bloody Sunday Inquiry began in March 2000. In June of 2001 the RUC had to protect pupils and parents at Holy Cross School in North Belfast. In October of the same year the IRA began decommissioning and a month later the RUC was replaced by the Police Service of Northern Ireland, recruiting on a 50/50 basis. During this period the new Assembly functioned or was dormant, dependent on progress with talks about decommissioning. In elections in November 2003 both Sinn Fein and the DUP made strong gains.

AREAS OF WORK

The work at Quaker House was entering a new phase and while concentrating on issues around the Parades and unrest relating to schools in interface areas in Belfast and Antrim, there were new opportunities for dialogue relating to the future of Northern Ireland with which Quaker House could engage. Mark, as a single Representative, had to focus on a limited range of issues. At the same time, the area around Quaker House was changing, with a rise in the number of student houses and a gradual deterioration of the physical environment.

Parades and Monitoring

This issue continued to cause major problems at certain times of the year. The levels of violence had dropped but Mark visited Drumcree to observe the parades and attended the service at Drumcree Church, taking the opportunity to talk with individuals. The same approach was adopted on the Ormeau Road and the

---

* Based on an interview with Mark Chapman 29.5.08. 108

Ardoyne, where he acted as an unofficial observer and responded where appropriate. He became involved as a monitor for Mediation Northern Ireland and the Belfast Interface Project working on the Short Strand and Newtownards Road interface for several months. He was able to talk with people on both sides where houses were being attacked by petrol bombs thrown by people linked to political factions. Quaker House was involved with another Mediation Northern Ireland project in Antrim, at the interface between two schools. Monitors were trained, as with Short Strand, being highly visible, wearing tabards, using walkie talkies, providing cover on a rota, looking out for trouble makers and liaising with the police and the schools. The process in Antrim eventually led to a solution where pupils were let out of school at different times to avoid potential conflict. The situation at Holy Cross School, where police were escorting pupils and their parents onto school premises over the summer of 2001 reflected the tensions within the neighbourhoods where loyalist and nationalist areas both felt under threat. Mark visited people in both areas. His previous links enabled him to bring a small group of republican and loyalist paramilitaries to Quaker House to discuss the situation.

Engagement of Quakers in Policy Consultations

Quaker House engaged in a collaborative activity using the resources of the recently formed organisation Community Dialogue. The Committee felt that it would be helpful for Quakers to engage with some of the emerging issues, especially with the parts of the Good Friday Agreement proposed by the politicians but not necessarily accepted by local people, e.g., policing and decommissioning and the early release of prisoners, despite the feelings of their victims' families. Meetings were held at Quaker House on a monthly basis with a group of Quakers listening and talking with loyalists and republicans about the issues. The para-militaries welcomed the opportunity to talk about the issues and Quakers were able to engage with the problems facing Northern Ireland in more detail. A recurring theme in these discussions was concern about the tensions in the Ulster Unionist Party over decommissioning and the way in which David Trimble was being undermined by other party members. A further concern was about the potential for instability following the 2001 Census which showed a growing percentage of Catholics in the population which fed Unionist fears that parties promoting a United Ireland could have majority support in an election. Further sessions were organised for local Friends to discuss 'A Shared Future' (a consultation paper on improving relations in Northern Ireland) and the Bill of Rights proposed by the Northern Ireland Human Rights Commission. Papers were submitted to both these consultations.

Peace Groups and Churches

Mark was involved with INNATE in its programme to bring the Alternatives to Violence Project (AVP) to Northern Ireland, taking part in training and prisoners work in Dublin. Although they were unable to take this forward within the prisons in Northern Ireland at the time, it was later taken up by UQSC who initiated discussions with Maghaberry Prison (see Chapter 3). Involvement with Quaker Peace Committee's work continued and included opposition to the invasion of Iraq. Mark also represented Friends in the meetings of the Churches Initiative Group of the Irish Council of Churches.

GOVERNANCE

Quaker House had been established and underwritten by QPS in Britain Yearly Meeting (BYM) but during Mark's tenure, responsibility was transferred to Ireland YM with Britain making a commitment to give an annual grant for some years. The newly constituted Quaker House Belfast Management Committee recognised that they would have a fundraising role. The immediate impact on Mark included an increase in work supporting the Committee and changes to his contract from a volunteer to salaried staff member. It took time to clarify his terms and conditions of service as he changed from being a volunteer with a large organisation to employment by a new committee which itself needed support. The added responsibility was equally difficult for the Committee, but it was very supportive of its Representative during this period of transition.

REFLECTIONS

Mark's time as Representative was during a period of new birth for Northern Ireland. The political landscape had opened up and there was no longer the same need for a space for off the record meetings of the type that had taken place at Quaker House in the past. The ceasefire was not complete but there was a reduced level of violence and people had more access to politicians. He felt that there were limitations to his work because he was appointed as the only Representative and would have welcomed the presence of a colleague to share ideas, although members of the Committee and his line manager fulfilled some of this role. The area in which Quaker House was located deteriorated.

The Committee undertook a review of the project and looked at its future direction. It concluded that the work of Quaker House had been effective and that there was still a need for the project, but with a changed emphasis. There was now a range of reconciliation groups actively engaged in Northern Ireland. Quaker House had had a role in starting or supporting some of these. Mark experienced a sense of satisfaction when working cooperatively with some of these organisations which over the years had become increasingly professional in their structures and programmes.

There was an eight month gap between Mark's departure and the arrival of his successor.

ANNE BENNETT
August 2004 - May 2007
Anne had retired from full time international work for Quakers and had a long term connection with Northern Ireland and with Quaker House. She was appointed as the Representative and lived in Quaker House on her own.

Northern Ireland 2004-2007

This period was marked with hopes of IRA decommissioning, improved relationships with the South and economic renewal, but uncertainty about the willingness of the DUP and Sinn Fein to work together as the largest parties in the newly elected Assembly. Hopes for the future were set against suspicion, years of violence and lack of trust. Issues around victims with unresolved problems from the past were emerging. A rapid rise in the numbers of immigrants from the new accession states of the EU combined with reports of numerous incidents of racist violence earned Belfast the dubious title of 'racist capital of Europe' in a popular newspaper.

AREAS OF WORK

The programme of work focussed on three areas: dealing with the past; the current issues of racism relating to the influx of migrant workers; and exploration of the issues facing Northern Ireland in the future. Initially Anne met with Mark Chapman building links with previous contacts of Quaker House and she also had the benefit of Steve Williams, an earlier Representative, as her line manager during her first year as she developed her programme.

Anti-Racism Work

The rise in racist attacks, sometimes mirroring the sectarian attacks of the past and the incidence of racist comments and discrimination was of concern to politicians, community and church leaders. Anne joined with groups addressing racism and became the Quaker member of the Embrace committee, an ecumenical group committed to publicizing immigration issues, relating to relevant government officials and offering assistance to individual immigrants and their families. She also represented Quakers on an ecumenical body developing a similar programme among the churches throughout Ireland. She formed close links with Muslim groups and organised a day conference on racism for Quakers, with speakers from several minority ethnic groups talking about their personal experiences of racism and racist attacks. This was well attended with representatives from most of the Quaker Meetings in Ulster. Out of this successful conference grew the Quaker House Anti Racism Group with representatives from six Quaker Meetings and the UQSC. It met regularly, produced a Newsletter distributed to all Meetings in Ulster, giving news, information and suggested opportunities for action. It supported the activities of individual Quakers and provided practical assistance of food and voluntary help for organisations working with refugees and immigrant workers. Links were maintained with Quakers in the South working on similar issues

Dialogue

Following Quaker House's involvement with the consultation process of the 'Shared Future' document, it seemed appropriate to develop a discussion programme to engage individuals. A group of up to 8 people drawn from Protestant and Catholic backgrounds came together with Anne and Steve Williams to discuss contentious issues facing Northern Ireland. They identified policing, education and housing for discussion, issues where opinions were often divided along sectarian lines. This group of strong individuals participated honestly and courageously over 10 sessions. They met a year later to review the process and were pleased with the ways they had been able to take their experiences back into their own churches.

Dealing with the Past

Anne explored a number of ways in which Quaker House could develop a Dealing with the Past (DWP) programme, linking ex-paramilitary groups in Northern Ireland with Quaker projects with ex-combatants in the Former Yugoslavia, but this did not prove possible. At this time there was general opposition among victims of the conflict to a proposed TV programme. It was to be chaired by Archbishop Desmond Tutu and to involve victims from both sides of the community meeting attackers and was based on a model used in South Africa. Quaker House brought together representatives of victims' groups to monitor the programmes and discuss them afterwards, exploring ways in which their stories could be heard. The sessions were facilitated by Anne and Roberta Bacic, a Chilean living in Northern Ireland with extensive knowledge of Truth Commissions in various parts of the world. A follow up seminar was well attended by a range of community groups, ex-prisoners, victims, politicians and NGOs working in this area. It was facilitated by Roberta who explored with the participants different models of Truth Commissions and ways of finding a process that would be helpful in the current environment. This seminar was followed by a second several months later, pursuing in more detail some of the issues raised at the first seminar.

During this work Anne viewed an exhibition of quilts made by Relatives for Justice, a victims' group, each square of the quilt made by an individual or family to commemorate a loved one who had died during the Troubles. She spoke with other organisations and discovered that they had produced quilts, mosaics and paintings all with the same theme. Most were community groups, some of them representing victims, and she explored with them the possibility of holding an exhibition to display their work together and suggested that some of their members might come together to design and make a new quilt depicting their shared vision of the future. They supported this idea enthusiastically and as Roberta was involved with this work she was able to organise an international dimension to the exhibition, with quilts produced in many areas of conflict. Anne completed her service at Quaker House before this work came to fruition and Roberta was able to take it forward resulting in a major exhibition of quilts in Derry in spring 2008.* Anne's successor at Quaker House, Olive Hobson, continued the work with a new quilt, designed and produced by a small group of women from both communities.**

Churches, Peace and Community Groups

In addition to the areas of work identified above, the Representative maintained Quaker House's links with other churches, especially through the Churches Initiative Group. INNATE continued to meet at Quaker House and Anne developed links with local community groups working to prevent the further deterioration of the area around Quaker House. Her background in training and senior management brought opportunities to provide support and lead training sessions for organisations with which she was working.

Organisational Issues

This was a period of transition for the project. The Quaker House Belfast Management Committee had assumed full responsibility for the work towards the end of Mark Chapman's tenure. Anne Bennett was involved with developing the programme but was also drawn, even more than Mark, into supporting the Committee and assisting with fundraising, the sale and clearance of Quaker House and helping to find new premises. The Committee and previous Representatives had been engaged over many years in trying to achieve charitable status for Quaker House. Although the project was committed to finding peaceful ways forward in Northern Ireland, its aims and objectives did not fall within the Charity legislation's identified categories and therefore Quaker House was not eligible for charitable status. However, in 2004 the regulations were amended and charitable status was granted.

---

* Roberta organised a very successful exhibition, 'The Art of Survival, International and Irish Quilts' in Derry, 8 March - 19 April 2008.
** Quaker House worked with the small group to design and produce a quilt reflecting the original theme. In September 2008 the 'Shared Vision' quilt was launched, with cross party support, at the Parliament building at Stormont.

The deterioration of the area around University Road with 98% of the houses divided into multi-occupancy, mainly by students, and associated issues of noise, litter and problems with parking, led the Committee to consider the future of Quaker House. It was decided, after long and careful thought, to ask BYM to sell the house and to seek new premises in the centre of Belfast with easy access by public transport and availability of parking. The house was sold in 2006 and the Quaker House Belfast Project was relocated to an office in the centre of the city in November 2006, as it completed its quarter century.

CONCLUSIONS

The extensive records of this project alongside the interviews produced sufficient material for a book rather than this short chapter! Much of the detail, humour, frustrations, commitment and energy of those involved with the project has had to be omitted. The process has, however, provided an opportunity to look back and review not only its programme but also the strengths and weaknesses of this way of working. Quakers recognised that this flexible approach is vulnerable to internal and external influences and relies heavily on the ability of its Representatives and committee members to respond to the ever changing political situation.

An essential feature of Quaker House Belfast was the cooperation of British and Irish Friends. It was part of a triangle with political work being undertaken in London and Dublin. This was needed in the early stages of the project but as the political scene eased, there was more direct contact between the various players. The work became more centred in Belfast and its nature gradually changed. Representatives developed their own programmes, still based on the key aims and previous work but with freedom to respond quickly to events. The House was used initially for informal 'off the record' meetings linked with work across the communities but changes to the political situation eventually meant that there was no longer a need for this type of safe, secure environment in which to meet. Also there were a growing number of other organisations providing resources. The programme of Quaker House was able to respond to the changes. The Representatives built on previous work to the aims and objectives of the project but had the freedom to develop new initiatives.

REVIEWS AND EVALUATIONS

Recognising that peace making and peace building is slow, steady work which frequently manifests few indicators of success at the time and is difficult to assess, the Committee arranged for several reviews of the work of Quaker House. They included a major review in 1995 when Clem McCartney interviewed individuals and groups who were actual or potential users of Quaker House. The comments politicians and other stakeholders made to the evaluator give a flavour of the methods used by Representatives:

'(Quaker House)…provided a neutral space where it was possible to sit with opponents over…lunch, even at the height of the killings'.
[nationalist]

'Often members of a local party would be given the opportunity to present their views to people from Great Britain or the Republic of Ireland'. [unionist]

'They kept in touch when other larger parties … did not want to know us. They may not have agreed with us, but they recognized you had a point of view'. [member of a smaller party]

'They explore your views and ask, What if?'
[political party representative]

The evaluator commented:

'There had been considerable change to life politically, socially and economically during this period and it is possible that Quaker House made a contribution to the whole, offering a quiet, non judgemental space for individuals and groups to explore their own thinking and that of others.'

McCartney, C. 1995

The report concluded that, although there were reservations, most users and commentators thought there was a need for the project to continue in 1995. Some informants felt Quakers should be more assertive and have a stronger intermediary role, but others thought the flexible facilitator role was valuable and that there were organisations better equipped to mediate and negotiate solutions.

A review of the work in 1998 stated:

'The context may change the people involved, but the task is still the same. It is to help long term healing and reconciliation between commu-

116

nities recovering from years of conflict, offering the unique contribution of Quaker experience'.

QHB Internal Review 1998

A further review and committee planning session in 2002 was facilitated by Brandon Hamber, who has wide experience of working in conflict and post conflict situations. The objectives were reexamined and detailed tasks listed under each one. It was found that facilitating politicians to meet had become much less a feature of the work since the official Peace Process had begun, while watching for areas of potential conflict in local communities, joint working with other organisations and building international links had assumed more importance. There was a great need to involve people in cross community initiatives to embed peaceful relationships at all levels, but resistance to this among many groupings. The framework from this review informed the next phase of work.

COMMITTEE STRUCTURES

Although this history has concentrated on the work of the Representatives at Quaker House, the role of the Committee has been crucial – a fact emphasized by all of the Representatives. Drawn from Britain and Ireland they brought a mix of experience, contacts and perspectives on the political situation and this diversity was found useful when planning programmes. The project was initiated by QPS in London, with management later transferred to Ireland Yearly Meeting, based in Dublin. Irish, mainly local Friends provided a support group which became the Local Executive Group (LEG) under the revised structure. Local committee members were involved in meetings which the Representatives organised and were on hand when there were crises to offer advice, opinions on personal safety or views on how events might develop. Along with other local Friends, they came to weekly meetings for worship at the House and were available for cover when Quaker House residents were away. The project has benefited from a succession of knowledgeable, committed and enthusiastic committee members who have given much time and energy in support of the work and, without them, Quaker House would not have been able to sustain its work.

The project also benefited from a series of able Representatives who were committed to the demands of living on the job 7 days a week. Inevitably, there were many frustrations! Much of their time involved following up contacts and attending meetings, in the hope that they would open doors but knowing that many would come to nothing. They had to be ready to respond to openings as they arose and to adapt as the external situation changed. Whether from Northern Ireland, Britain or the USA,* they would have to overcome preconceptions about their views and try to become acceptable to all sides. The last two Representatives were appointed to work alone, leaving them devoid of immediate peer support and someone on hand to share the facilitation of meetings and discussion afterwards. As time went on, the original model of political work changed and other venues became acceptable for reconciliation work, so the house was no longer the focus of the work. This made it easier for the project to move when the physical environment around Quaker House deteriorated.

Reflection shows that useful elements of the Quaker House project were:

- A committed and flexible Management Committee able to mobilize support from the two Yearly Meetings (Britain and Ireland).
- A group of local people who are aware of the intricacies of the political/religious setting, able to provide a line manager, objective advice, and a sounding board (especially important for single workers.)
- Regular reviews of the project and learning from good practice elsewhere.
- Flexible, mature Representatives, able to maintain an overview of the political situation and respond, deal with disappointment, maintain a positive approach and a welcoming environment and keep their sense of humour!
- Recognition that the work is slow and time consuming and needs long term targets as well as short. Awareness of the opportunities and limitations of such work.
- Financial stability and clarity about fundraising. (As much of the early funding came from a number of Quaker charities, Quaker House itself was not seen as being in competition for funding with the organisations with whom it worked.)

---

* Of the 10 Representatives appointed during the 25 years, 3 were from Northern Ireland, 5 from Britain and 2 from the USA. It had been hoped that Quakers would be appointed from the South but this has yet to happen.

- Clarity about not expressing a view on the situation, but ready to listen to all views and with an ability to reflect back what is being heard, especially to opposing parties.
- Collaborative working – the need to build on relationships with groups who have similar aims, form partnerships and share resources. This is a common feature of the charity sector and among peace builders in Northern Ireland, as elsewhere.

Quaker House was established for a particular purpose but:

> *'While the levels of violence have largely disappeared and politics returns to something approaching normality, the need for reconciliation and peacebuilding is greater than ever at all levels in society. The Northern Ireland community still faces the twin tasks of dealing with our fractured past and addressing the challenge of creating a new, shared future.'*

QHB Report 1998

This brief history of the work of Quaker House during its first 25 years relates to the period July 1982 to May 2007. New Representatives were appointed and the work of the Quaker House Belfast continues.

References

Jones, Rufus (1937) in **Quaker Faith and Practice: The Book of Christian Discipline of the Yearly Meeting of the Religious Society of Friends (Quakers) in Britain 24.56:** BYM 1994.

McCartney, Clem (1995) **Impressions of Quaker House – the views of actual and potential users.** Quaker House Belfast (QHB) internal document.

Northern Ireland Committee (NIC) of Quaker Peace and Service London (QPS) (1984) **Report to QPS Central Committee.**

Quaker House Belfast (1983) **Statement to New Ireland Forum** 12/9/83 Internal document.

Quaker House Belfast (1998) **Internal Review** by Management Committee.

Quaker House Belfast Management Committee (1998) **Report to QPS** November 1998.

Quaker Peace and Service (1984) **Report to QPS Central Committee** January 1984.

Yarrow C. H., Mike (1978) **Quaker Experiences in International Conciliation** New Haven and London: Yale University Press.

Chapter 6

QUAKER PEACE EDUCATION PROJECT

Seamus Farrell

'If we are to reach real peace in the world, we shall have to begin with children'.
Mahatma Gandhi

PROJECT BEGINNINGS

FROM THE early 70s many Friends* had been concerned about the limited Quaker response to the outbreak of conflict in Northern Ireland. Their concern led to the establishment of the Ulster Quaker Service Committee (UQSC). By the end of the 1970s, UQSC had become very active indeed, with its work at the Visitors' Centre at the Maze Prison and other social action projects and had, by this stage, sourced substantial financial resources to fund their services (see Chapter 3). The Ulster Quaker Peace Committee (UQPC) was still a small voluntary committee with a budget of £100 and had already shown its interest in schools-related peace work by organising peace-poster competitions. When Coleraine Friend Andrew Young became a member, his involvement was to lead eventually to the establishment of the Quaker Peace Education Project (QPEP). The Peace Committee members were keen to be involved in work with schools or young people. Another Peace Committee member, Allen Pearson, is credited with raising the idea, but it was undoubtedly Andrew Young's energy and strategic thinking that proved significant. In June 1985, as Chairman of UQPC

---

* The word Friend is used inter-changeably with Quaker throughout this book.

121

and with the help of a working party, he organised a conference at Coleraine. The aim was to meet those already involved in peace education and find out whether there were any gaps which Quakers could try to fill. Representatives from the Department of Education, the Education and Library Boards, the Northern Ireland Curriculum Council and the University of Ulster were invited as were people from the Corrymeela Community, the Community Relations in Schools Project (CRIS), and the Peace People.

According to a subsequent report of the conference in *The Friendly Word* (TFW), Ireland's Quaker Journal, conference participants were of the opinion that:

> *'Quaker reputation for respecting the beliefs and attitudes of others would enable [them] to play an important part in Education for Mutual Understanding. It would be appropriate for Quakers to become active in peace education because we are seen by the community at large as being independent and are respected as such. We could attempt to do things which other groups might find more difficult'.*

TFW 1986

The response seemed to surprise Andrew Young. He subsequently told Jerry Tyrrell of QPEP that he had thought the participants might 'suggest that we ran a Peace Essay competition. I wasn't expecting a hundred-thousand pound project. But we'll do it' (Young 1993). Following the conference Andrew met from time to time with John Lampen and Clem McCartney who had some experience of conflict resolution. Together they produced a draft programme for moving forward, including a proposal for a full-time paid worker. Andrew insisted throughout that he was not a peace educator. He focused on the financial side of things. The same edition of 'The Friendly Word' provided an outline of the working party's vision for the project.

> *It is expected that a programme would develop performing some or all of the following functions:*

- *Collating and disseminating information on existing resources.*
- *Visiting schools and mounting events in schools in collaboration with teachers.*
- *Establishing on-going groups of like-minded teachers.*
- *Arranging the provision of skills-training for peace educators.*

- *Providing a measure of consultancy and feed-back to established and developing ventures.*
- *Researching the effectiveness of strategies already being employed in peace education.*
- *Identifying and developing untried strategies.*
- *Seeking to enter into dialogue with those hostile to peace education.*
- *Liaising with other groups developing peace education.*

TFW 1986

It is noteworthy too that the focus was on interaction with teachers and not on the production of curriculum materials. This latter need was being addressed by what was then known as the Joint Peace Education Programme (JPEP) of the Irish Council of Churches and the Irish Commission for Justice and Peace. The fact that JPEP was located in Belfast and had a sole staff member may also have been a reason for the decision to locate the project in the North West. Indeed it was envisaged that the project might help with the dissemination of Peace Education materials and with the training that was needed to go with them in the West of the Province since Norman Richardson of JPEP could not easily cover all of Northern Ireland. The working party envisaged a strong partnership between the two projects.

The linking of the Project with the University of Ulster was entirely the initiative and achievement of Andrew Young. He had substantial contacts there, having recently retired as Professor of Mathematics. Negotiations between UQPC and the University were protracted. They concluded with agreement that the Project would become an action-research project of the University's Centre for the Study of Conflict and be located at the Magee campus in Derry*. A lot of attention was given to the formation of the management committee. A central concern was how to meet the needs of both Quakers and the University – each of whom would have had the same basic aims but possibly divergent methods. Somewhat to the surprise of the Quaker negotiators, the University did not want to be the majority group on the management committee and they specifically wanted a Quaker to be chairperson.

In the end it was decided to have 4 Quaker representatives and 3 University people on the Committee. The four Quakers were

---

* Also known as Londonderry. Both names are used in this chapter.

John Lampen (chairperson), Alec McEwan and Felicity Boyd of UQPC and John Murray, a Quaker who was also a member of staff of the Western Education and Library Board but the Board authorities made it very clear that, while it supported the Project, John was not on the Committee as its representative. The Education for Mutual Understanding (EMU) programme, which was later to become a statutory component of the Northern Ireland Curriculum, was only beginning at that time and was not official policy; indeed it was a matter of considerable political sensitivity. Initially the representatives from the University were Professor John Darby, Director of the Centre of the Study of Conflict, and Dr. Stephen Ryan, Senior Lecturer in Peace Studies. When John Darby retired from the Centre, his successor, Professor Seamus Dunn, joined the Management Committee. For the reasons indicated earlier Norman Richardson of JPEP was also asked to become a member.

Meantime Andrew Young was combining incredible energy with his particular skills in fund-raising to ensure that the project could get under way. By the time the staff had been appointed in April 1988 he had either raised the funds or secured promises of sufficient resources for the first three years. Quaker individuals, and Meetings throughout Ireland and Britain contributed most generously. While other sources including the Ireland Fund and the Commission of the European Community provided funding, the bulk of donations were from Quaker individuals, Meetings, and Trusts, in particular the Joseph Rowntree Charitable Trust.

Andrew continued to give his time, energy and ability to fund-raising and keeping accounts for the project until his untimely death in 1993. As chairman of the UQPC he was happy to leave the running of the project to the Management Committee, all the while insisting that he personally knew nothing about peace education. When to fund-raising is added his pivotal role in linking the project with the University, and in doing so bringing to it a significant standing and substantial support – as well as numerous advantages in terms of fund-raising – his contribution to the Project, and to the UQPC, was inestimable.

THE PROJECT GETS UNDER WAY

The appointment in April 1988 of Jerry Tyrrell as Project Director proved to be a stroke of either good luck or genius, and more likely a combination of the two. A qualified teacher from London, he came to Northern Ireland under the auspices of the Fellowship of Reconciliation. He had hoped to secure a teaching post in Derry but was unsuccessful. After a short period of unemployment however he began work as the Organiser of Holiday Projects West, an initiative of individuals including teachers who were concerned at the impact on children of the chaos and tension prevailing in the areas where they lived.

Jerry relates how he came to QPEP:

Initially I was put off by the job title 'Research Assistant'....I saw research as being dry and academic. But once I saw the job specification and the whole thing about supporting teachers, peace education, being a resource etc., I saw that there was scope for everything I wanted to do.... About 18 months prior to getting the job I had been in the States and I'd been seeing ways in which training in nonviolence had been adapted into a classroom setting and I was very excited by that. I saw this job therefore as a vehicle for me to do what I had seen done. One of the things in the job specification which caught my eye immediately was that part of the job was to speak to people who were hostile to peace education. I found it an interesting notion – not just preaching to the converted.

Tyrrell, J. 1993

John Lampen, an English Friend living in Londonderry at this time, was chair of the Management Committee for four years. He was himself an experienced teacher and also played an active role as a QPEP team member. Not being in full-time paid employment he had the time to devote to the Project that none of the other Committee members had.

Staff Members and Volunteers

The other two people employed on the Project were Sharon Moran (Resources Administrator), who following the death of Andrew Young also did the accounts, and Eileen Healy (Programme Manager). Such a small staff would have had limited impact and consideration was given in the initial planning to the possibility of securing extra staff through the ACE Scheme.* Jerry brought with

---

* Action for Community Employment (ACE), a Northern Ireland government job creation scheme.

him from Holiday Projects a very positive experience and a strong conviction about the potential of volunteers. He was aware that there were many people who, through their involvement in similar areas, had a lot of skills with young people and who didn't have jobs. Availing of their services meant that the Project was able to make a bigger impact on more schools. Within a very short time he had put together a team of volunteers, trained with the help of the Ways and Means manual of Kingston Friends (from Kingstonupon-Thames, Surrey), who were doing specific focused work in schools. Local volunteers were augmented from the beginning and over the years by members of a German reconciliation organisation Eirene and by links with Earlham College in Richmond Indiana, USA, which provided part-time placement students. Jerry, with strong support from John Lampen, put great emphasis on the training of volunteers, on continuous rehearsal and practice and on good planning.

Like most strengths, however, the volunteer programme had its downside. Vetting was inadequate and insufficient attention was paid to issues such as dress and being sensitive to the dynamics of schools and the needs of teachers. The volunteer programme relied rather heavily on the tolerance and goodwill of teachers and more specifically on Jerry's personality and the trust that he built up with schools. Perhaps because everyone has been to school there is a tendency on the part of outsiders to be less sensitive about engaging with teachers than, for example, with the staff of a hospital operating theatre! In addition teachers, conditioned by spending most of every day as the sole adult among a group of children and very conscious of their responsibility to manage behaviour, can be understandably discomforted by having several visitors (nonteachers) engaging with their children in highly interactive processes – and leaving the teacher to 'pick up the pieces'! Nor did it help that some volunteers brought with them considerable negativity to schools on account of their own personal experiences as children.

EDUCATION FOR MUTUAL UNDERSTANDING

Prior to QPEP's establishment the term 'Education for Mutual Understanding' (EMU) had emerged to describe efforts by committed teachers and voluntary bodies in Northern Ireland to engage with the formal education sector in respect of the conflict.

In Britain the term 'Peace Education' had come to appear synonymous with the activities of the Campaign for Nuclear Disarmament (CND). An alternativew term 'Community Relations Education' left practitioners open to suspicions of social engineering – whether towards a united Ireland or towards assimilating Nationalists into the Northern Ireland state. EMU was formally adopted by the Department of Education in 1983 – the year that QPEP began. Over the years, with QPEP as a major contributor, EMU gained credibility and became part of the curriculum from late 1989 onwards, together with a related theme of Cultural Heritage. The statutory provisions relating to these educational themes came into operation in 1992.

So QPEP began at a time when EMU had gained formal recognition but as to the how, what, when, where and/or why of it there was a plethora of ideas, together with continued resistance to the very notion of it. This then was the context in which the original objectives were developed (see above Project Beginnings). For Jerry Tyrrell the range of QPEP's functions was best summarised by one of these, 'Identifying and developing untried strategies'.

First Engagement with Schools

Jerry made the best possible use of the contacts that he had established with teachers and others during his time at Holiday Projects and the strong links that members of the Management Committee had with education in general and EMU in particular. He very quickly embarked on a programme of visits to principals of schools. The invitation that provided the first opportunity for QPEP to work with children came from Rosemount Primary School, whose Principal was aware of the historical role of Quakers in peace education. Less than three months into the life of the Project it responded to that invitation with workshops for Primary 5 and 6 children on the themes of affirmation, cooperation and communication. Simultaneous negotiations with the Model Primary school resulted in parallel workshops there. An opportunity arose to bring the children of both schools together at the Corrymeela Community's Centre in Ballycastle for a residential experience – with positive outcomes and considerable learning for both the Project and the schools. In March of 1989 QPEP linked with Dr. Alan Smith at the Centre for the Study of Conflict for a major

EMU project with 3 primary schools in Limavady. A significant and successful innovation in this venture was the involvement of parents. The work was written up as part of the Extending School Links project (Smith & Dunn 1990).

A programme which greatly enhanced the profile of QPEP in primary schools in the city of Derry was the 'Primary 7 Conference'. It was John Lampen's idea to acknowledge the value of children's ideas, and to give them a forum to address issues that concerned them. The format of a 6th form conference was replicated to give similar status to the event; each school sent a number of delegates, aged eleven, and the conference took place at an outside venue. There was a consistently high turn out from the schools at what became an annual event. This greatly helped the Project to become known in all the schools and to be identified for its respect for and trust in children. This was particularly so when delegates were able to feed back their experiences to principals, teachers and their peers; they invariably created a very favourable impression. The theme of the first Conference, in May 1989, was 'Your City in the Year 2000'. The venue was the city's Guildhall and the day culminated in a press conference! In May 1991 the production of a wall 'newspaper' entitled 'The New World' and dated 1996 carried news reports of 'A World without Weapons' and was the outcome of the Conference of that name. Children's growing sense of ownership of their conference informed the decision in 1992 to address an area of obvious concern to participants, namely transition from primary to secondary school. Some participants of previous P7 Conferences devised and presented role-play scenarios based on their experiences of going up to secondary school. The theme of bullying at a subsequent conference led to the proceedings being published as part of a chapter in a book 'Countering Bullying' edited by Delwyn Tattum and Graham Herbert (Lampen & Farrell 1990).

Initial Engagement with Adults

As well as work with children the Project quickly sought to reach and support teachers working in isolation and to arrange skills-training for them and other adults. An early initiative, in conjunction with the Workers Educational Association, provided a course of five evening workshops for 'teachers, youth workers, community workers ... involved or interested in EMU' (WEA 1988).

Kingston Friends Workshop Group – Approaches to Peace Education

Experiences of Quaker peace education initiatives around the world had been impressively accumulated and built upon by the Kingston Friends Workshop Group. The Group was the single most important resource for the Project in terms of the theoretical framework at the heart of its approach to peace education, and the games and activities that it used in its interactive teaching methodologies. Sue Bowers, co-founder of Kingston Friends Workshop Group and co-author of its peace education manual 'Ways and Means – An Approach to Problem Solving' (Bowers 1984), was particularly influential in QPEP's early development. Support and guidance also came from the Education and Advisory Service of Quaker Peace and Service (QPS) in London and continued throughout the Project's existence. Also worth mentioning is the support from West Midlands Quaker Peace Education Project in England.

There is a need to deal with the underlying factors. In a conflict situation these are non-cooperation, deficits in communication and a lack of self-esteem and appreciation of others. Skills in affirmation, communication and cooperation are central to relationships – and their deficiency is central to conflict. As with an iceberg, 90% of which is below the surface, the visible aspect of a conflict is not the whole of it. Efforts to solve a conflict by dealing only with the visible part is like trying to decapitate an iceberg – the only outcome will be that a new iceberg appears.

In terms of process and methodology QPEP had inherited a strong belief in the importance of creating a safe, participative and cooperative environment during workshops – for participants of any age. In the case of one-off workshops with children, participants were asked at the beginning to agree to a standard set of ground rules, which over a period were refined and enhanced as a result of the comments of children. But where a series of workshops were being offered, the Project made use of the time-frame available to request their teachers to engage with the children in prior development of an Agreement that would ensure that everyone would feel safe and enjoy their participation in the workshop.

It is worth considering the significance of this practice – as an example of how QPEP acted as a catalyst for substantial change in thinking and practice within formal education and beyond. What

129

may seem like a minor variation was, strategically, quite subversive. Besides being a way of engaging the teachers, at a deeper level it was a challenge to them to move outside the convention in schools where rules are prescribed, and to take the risk of trusting the children by engaging with them in a negotiated agreement process to identify the prerequisites for a happy workshop. Teachers who did this found that the suggestions of the children were for the most part reasonable and indeed creative and that those that weren't could be used as a learning and discussion point. In particular they noted how, as a result of the process, the children's sense of ownership and responsibility for ensuring a happy environment for all greatly enhanced the workshop experience and the learning from it. The fact that their teachers and QPEP people also agreed to abide by their agreement delighted and surprised the children. QPEP made a point throughout the workshops of keeping the Agreement to the fore. As a result of the experience many teachers opted for negotiating agreements in their classrooms in preference to prescribed ground rules. They used the same participative process as for the workshops and likewise they were themselves parties to the agreement. The significance of such change, in respect of teacher/pupil relationships and by extension of whole-school relationships can hardly be underestimated. And at a societal level it lays foundations for responsible citizenship and participatory democracy based on trust and respect.

QPEP began very quickly to emerge as a significant contributor to thinking and practice in the field of peace education. With the experience of working in a deeply conflictual environment, the Project was able not just to affirm the relevance of the commonly agreed theoretical framework to its own context, but also to argue that it should not be supplanted by any pressure or perceived need for engagements which are more visibly connected to the specifics of a conflict. While it would be appropriate subsequently to help senior secondary school students to engage with such specifics, the Project felt that even in this case, preliminary work was essential around communication, cooperation and affirmation of self and others. In the case of primary children it discouraged the involvement of children in adult issues and focused on work with children around their own issues, friends falling out, name-calling, bullying and so on.

NEW STRATEGY: RESPONSE TO A DIVIDED EDUCATION SYSTEM

The conflict in Northern Ireland has been commonly depicted as a clash of cultures, between those claiming British identity and those seeking recognition of their Irish identity. To this cultural diversity dynamic has frequently been added the Christian denominational diversity – that between those of Protestant denominations and those of the Roman Catholic one. The fact that, except for a small minority, children of each tradition were schooled separately right through to completion of secondary schooling, inevitably led to many initiatives to enable children from both traditions to experience being with each other. It also explains the formal establishment of the close relationship between the educational themes of EMU and Cultural Heritage (CH).

In 1987 statutory support became available for cross-community contact programmes between schools. But, despite the potential value of such experiences, the availability of funding and the dedication of many of the adults involved to mutual understanding, the overall outcomes of this early work was questionable. Often preparation for the encounter was minimal, content was organised by venue staff and the accompanying teachers were not required to engage in the sessions. Planning was sometimes limited to a few phone calls between the school Principals or EMU co-ordinators. There may have been no contact between children for the rest of the year even when partner schools were not, as was frequently the case, geographically distant from one another. The outcomes for building peace and mutual understanding were therefore often limited.

While seeking to support good practice in cross-community contact, QPEP opted not to become specifically identified with these programmes. In a keynote address which Jerry Tyrrell delivered in Autumn 1988 he argued strongly for maintaining a focus on the development in children of values and skills in the areas of affirmation, cooperation and communication and:

'...working with children to deal with the everyday conflicts in [children's] lives, before even beginning to incorporate the added complication of dealing with the 'other tradition'.

Tyrrell, J. 1988

In the same address he spoke of the Project's specific identification with the EMU objective of:

'learning the importance of resolving difference and conflict by peaceful and creative means'.

Tyrrell, J. 1988

The Project however did provide support where it saw the possibility of having a strategic impact. Such an opportunity arose in 1992 when it was approached to work with three local primary schools, located within walking distance of each other but in community relations terms very distant indeed from each other. Teachers involved readily acknowledged that very little contact had been achieved on previous shared school outings. They had arranged that the children would travel together to the venue but there was no mixing on the bus. QPEP conducted a series of workshops with the three schools, following which the children collaborated happily and excitedly in decision making and task allocation during a joint educational trip to the local railway museum. This particular engagement was significant for the active involvement of the teachers in planning and delivery of the workshops. Previously the Project took responsibility for both design and delivery of its work. The effectiveness of this particular piece of collaboration made the Project more determined to develop a partnership and co-leadership relationship with teachers and schools.

Another example of how the Project used the Department of Education's Cross-community Contact Scheme very effectively was when it was asked to facilitate an innovative venture involving the recently opened Oakgrove Integrated Primary School[*] and Belmont House – a school for children with special needs. Since both schools catered for children from both main communities, the venture did not in itself qualify for assistance under the Cross-community Contact Scheme. But by using 6th form students from local State and Catholic schools as co-facilitators, the programme did qualify for a grant under the scheme – and, more importantly, it provided leadership opportunities for the 6th formers in the context of working together. The focus of this chapter until now has been on the Project's engagements at primary school level – the progression from work with children to also working with

---

[*] See Glossary for Integrated Education.

teachers, and towards partnership with teachers in the provision of children's workshops. In fact the most substantial and most effective work done by the Projects was at primary school level, although the Project also worked in Secondary level schools.

Secondary Level Experience

In the first year a venture was initiated with the hope of involving 4th Year students coming together from a State and a Catholic Secondary School in the Waterside area of Derry but it was not to be. In 1988 QPEP undertook to teach peace studies to 6th form students at Foyle and Londonderry College – an engagement that was to continue for four years. It had a mandatory element at the beginning but as it became more optional the young people came to enjoy the informality of the approach and began more and more to address issues of concern to them. It developed to the point where the young people themselves led the workshops towards the end of the ten-week course. But although located within the College there was no staff involvement and it had little impact beyond the course itself.

In 1992 QPEP responded to an invitation from St Columb's College in Derry to work with its entire teaching staff to develop a conflict resolution unit within its Pastoral Care programme. The head of sixth form who first approached QPEP about the venture subsequently reported that:

It had been the most enjoyable and worthwhile Baker Day [In Service Training] that the participants had ever been involved in.
Rainey, J. 1993, QPEP Annual Report

Teachers acknowledged the relevance of the workshop approach and content which was very innovative in the environment of secondary schools. It became clear however that further engagement with this initiative would have tied up the Project's entire resources and staff time. The experience generated useful thinking about engaging more strategically and strengthened QPEP's resolve to make the involvement of teachers in every aspect of a programme a prerequisite to any work with children.

When, soon after, an invitation was received to work with an entire year group of 4th formers at another school for the purposes of 'promoting co-operation and understanding among them

133

in preparation for their final year at school' the work began in the staff-room. Teachers with 4th form teaching or pastoral care responsibilities took part in all the workshops. A three-week gap between workshops allowed for the processing of evaluations and feedback, bringing this into a meeting with teachers. The programme challenged the notion of EMU as something to be 'done onto' young people by adults who don't themselves need to engage with the issues. The meetings with teachers were important mutual learning experiences as Project and school staff worked together on dilemmas and problems that arose. Teachers had very legitimate fears about the level of sharing which the Project seemed to be requiring from participants and how this might make them vulnerable subsequently:

> *Proposals by the Project envisaged sharing with each other much more deeply about themselves than usual. The fear was expressed that students who did take this risk could have it used against them by others subsequently and that a dread about this happening would create a mood of resistance to the whole process.*
>
> Farrell, S. 1991/2, QPEP Annual Report

Learning Sensitivity and Engaging with Resistance

In the first few years the Project may have been, as mentioned earlier, somewhat insensitive to the dynamics of schools and the concerns of teachers, in particular as regards its use of volunteers. This was especially true at secondary level, where there was a perception of the Project as well-meaning but lacking the necessary professionalism for working at that level. For the Project the 4th form venture constituted a very steep learning curve. It emphasised the importance of teachers not being left to deal with unnecessary difficulties in consequence of the less formal environment and more interactive dynamics of QPEP workshops compared to the normal pattern of classroom functioning. Some of the resistance which the Project encountered in school settings in its earlier years was not without justification. At the same time some resistance was inevitable because it constituted a challenge to the comfort zones of some teachers. The work required an interactive, workshop approach, with teachers and other adults sitting in a circle as equal participants with the children. Many teachers found it difficult to cope with the lack of visible hierarchical status. Some of the resistance at that level might have been overcome with more sensitivity. Underlying the practical differences between the workshop environment and the traditional confines of a classroom, was the challenge to teachers to explore new forms of working with and new ways of relating to children. As such it touched on very sensitive issues indeed.

There was resistance, too, to the very notion of peace education and EMU and especially of the kind being advocated by QPEP

– which sought not just teachers' presence in work with children but their willingness to consider their own emotions and opinions with respect to the 'other' community and to other issues of diversity. The notion that peace education was something to be delivered to children was quite prevalent among teachers, reflecting a denial process which posited that teachers are somehow immune to the prejudices of their respective communities in respect of others, and are therefore immediately able to teach mutual understanding and tolerance. Another evasive strategy was to argue that a school's responsibility to provide EMU could be met through the engagement of those teachers who have an interest in it, leaving other teachers, as well as whole-school issues of ethos, policy and practice, unaffected. Denial among teachers merely reflected that within the whole adult community. Teachers were somehow expected to be able to counter the prejudices and attitudes being constantly imbibed by children from their respective communities when not at school! While continually asserting the importance of peace education in schools the Project insisted that 'Education cannot compensate for society' (Bernstein 1970, p.38).

Because of its focus on work with children and young people, the adults with whom the Project had primary engagement were educators and, besides the in-service training provision referred to above, QPEP also worked regularly in teacher training institutions. It also hosted the first Summer School of the European Network for Conflict Resolution in Education (ENCORE) at the Magee Campus of the University of Ulster, 18-22 July 1992. A key contributor to ENCORE was Julian Weissglass whose theory of educational change identified emotional support for teachers as a critical ingredient in educational change (Weissglass 1991). He proposed a 'Dyad' exercise through which individual teachers can have the opportunity for emotional discharge in the presence of an individual of his or her choice, the role of the latter being simply to listen with neither criticism nor approval. It was offered by QPEP to teachers at in-service training sessions and adopted by many of them.

APPLICATION OF OTHER MODELS AND INTERNATIONAL LINKS

The issue of prejudicial attitudes and practice, at individual and group levels, was clearly an underpinning dynamic in the Northern Ireland conflict and Jerry was anxious to find a process that could be used by the Project – with teachers, youth workers and senior secondary school students, and also with the wider adult community, to address these issues. In February 1988 he participated in a 'Prejudice Reduction' Training of Trainers workshop provided by the National Coalition Building Institute (NCBI) in the USA. As a result of this, six similar annual workshops, also facilitated by the NCBI, were organised in Northern Ireland. Although some participants were enthusiastic about this model of work and its application, others had reservations, particularly about the personal disclosure of painful experiences encouraged during the workshops with no follow up to provide support afterwards. Some felt there were risks in transposing a model developed for an American society where people might be more comfortable with sharing intimate details of their life story, to Northern Ireland where the cultural norms were different. As NCBI were not able to agree to adapt the programme for the different context, it was decided not to continue with training adult facilitators to use this model for prejudice reduction and the team learnt something about the need to culturally adapt programmes which was useful to them in future international work.

Quaker Peace and Service (QPS) brought a delegation from the Soviet Peace Committee to look at peace-building projects in Northern Ireland in 1990. While in Derry they watched a QPEP children's workshop; John Lampen subsequently led peace education work programmes in Belarus and Ukraine which involved QPEP members of staff Eileen Healy and Sharon Moran and volunteer Tanya Gallagher at various times. A visit to Londonderry by a Ugandan peace builder, Nelson Onono-Oweng (now Anglican Bishop of Gulu), led to the peace education programme of the Fellowship of Reconciliation (Jamii ya Kupatanisha) in Uganda, to which Jerry Tyrrell and John Lampen went at different times on training visits. Nelson subsequently received the annual UNESCO Peace Education Prize. These and the hosting of the ENCORE Summer School in 1992 led to a growing number of international contacts for the Project.

QPEP: AN ACTION/RESEARCH PROJECT OF THE UNIVERSITY

As indicated earlier, QPEP had the status of an action-research project at the University of Ulster's Centre for the Study of Conflict, which gave it considerable kudos, accommodation in University premises at the Magee Campus and access to a range of University resources. It must be acknowledged however, that the Project did not exactly fit the definition of a university research project. The Joseph Rowntree Charitable Trust, which was QPEP's principal funder from the beginning, stipulated very specifically that they didn't want it to become just another academic research project. They wanted it to be a hands-on, practical project. They didn't want Jerry and others to get distracted into writing yet more papers. And neither did Jerry; he wanted above all to be a practitioner.

Academics and practitioners do not have a particularly good track record in terms of mutual understanding and collaboration and it is difficult to find someone who can embody both perspectives. Jerry was a good practitioner and with his enthusiasm and people skills, he was an excellent motivator and trainer of others. It can be argued strongly that this is what EMU and teachers in Northern Ireland schools most needed – methodologies of immediate value in the classroom and support to develop the confidence and competence to use them. At the initial Conference at Coleraine in 1985 there had been a strong consensus among teachers present that it should not be set up to produce more curriculum materials, already being produced by the Churches' Joint Peace Education Project. They wanted something else. Teachers had been mandated to teach EMU as a cross-curricular theme but had not been told how. By working with children in partnership with teachers, demonstrating that its approaches work and helping teachers to use them, the quality of EMU delivery was hugely enhanced. That contribution could have been further enhanced by the application of an academic focus. But there have been projects designed with intellectual rigour to function as a 'horse' that have turned out to be a 'camel'!

Jerry was therefore faced on the one hand with the pressures of a university institution and all that that implies, and on the other hand with the requirements of the funders who were giving him another agenda. But in truth his heart lay with the focus of the funders! As his Line Manager and Director of the Centre for the Study of Conflict, Seamus Dunn continued to try to get him to think in terms of the intellectual side of what he was doing, to try to analyse and bring some critical argument and evaluation to the work being done. And the Project created difficulties for Dunn at university level; his attention was drawn on occasions by University colleagues to Project materials appearing as University publications which were seriously deficient as pieces of academic writing. His tolerance and support deserve acknowledgement. The Project's link to the University was hugely advantageous to it and it would have achieved much less otherwise.

PROJECT EVALUATION

The Project had been deficient in terms of on-going evaluation but as it was drawing to a close a serious effort was made to draw learning from its work. The Charities Evaluation Service (CES) was contracted to conduct an external evaluation of the Project's impact and possibilities of development, funded by Joseph Rowntree Charitable Trust and a Quaker legacy – the Jessie Cairns Bequest. The evaluation was begun in June 1993 by CES Evaluator Jim O'Neill. A practical motivation was the need to have an evaluation:

'in anticipation of Government proposals over what funding would be available for voluntary projects'.

Boyd, F. 1992,

QPEP Minutes O'Neill conducted very extensive interviews with the range of stakeholders and this author transcribed the tapes of interviews. O'Neill presented a draft evaluation report to the QPEP Management Committee in October 1993 and, after receiving comments, the final evaluation in December 1993. Not surprisingly the Evaluation found that:

'Not enough ongoing evaluation was carried out within QPEP which could have provided more self-critical analysis and help set priorities'.

O'Neill, J. 1993, 1.3.4

Jerry readily accepted this conclusion and, writing subsequently, he acknowledged that the Project had been workshop driven. Although a few weekend evaluations had taken place in the course of the Project:

'The time needed to reflect on the learnings from [these] evaluations was not created, [as a result of which] at times mistakes were repeated or there wasn't the time to try out new ideas and approaches, depending instead on tried and tested ones'.

Tyrrell, J. 1995

He did not however as willingly accept the Evaluation's findings that:

'A lot of energy and resources were put into the work with other agencies which could have been better utilised in working more with schools'.

O'Neill, J. 1993, 1.3.2

One context of this finding was Jerry's interest in working in prisons and in introducing the Alternatives to Violence (AVP) Project in Northern Ireland, a project that had emanated from the work of Quakers with prisoners in the New York State prison system. He had sought from the Management Committee and been given permission to take part in a few pilot schemes in prisons but was told not to take on an on-going commitment there. His reaction to the Evaluation finding reveals that he would love to have been able to transcend the confines of formal education and have a menu of engagements! Overall, the Evaluation strongly recommended that the work of the Project should be continued and that all concerned should come together to formulate strategic plans, and to have funding applications ready for submission before the end of the present Project's lifespan. Not surprisingly it recommended that any follow-up project should commit to on-going self-evaluation to enable it to monitor the achievement of targets and set priorities.

THE PEER MEDIATION PILOT PROJECT

The Evaluation specifically recommended that the work begun to develop in the field of conflict resolution should be continued. Early in the Project, Eileen Healy produced 'Wee People' a booklet of conflict resolution skills which proved a very popular resource for teachers. A pilot peer mediation project was started concurrently with the Evaluation and had very positive feedback. This and the Project's other experiences of helping children deal with conflict as part of its support for EMU led to further development towards training children in concrete skills of negotiation and mediation. The 1993 P7 Conference was devoted to the theme of 'Peer Mediation' and a brochure entitled 'Conflict Busters' (Lampen 1993) was distributed to participants. The Principals of the Model Primary School and Oakgrove Integrated Primary School, impressed by the enthusiastic feedback provided by the schools' delegates to the Conference, responded to an invitation to all primary schools in Londonderry to participate in a pilot peer mediation project.

The venture provided both opportunity and demand for a more focused engagement than previously on structured research and evaluation. After each workshop the children's evaluations were collated into a usable form for the planning of the next one. As the workshops progressed, children responded to carefully designed questions which enabled the facilitators to obtain indications as to the learning acquired, gaps in the learning and the needs of participants. Classroom work, for each of the periods between workshops, was examined and fed back into the subsequent planning. Regular discussions were held with the teachers and the Principals. QPEP Team planning and rehearsal in advance of each workshop was rigorous. All of the Primary 7 children in each school were offered a series of six 105-minute workshops held weekly between October and December 1993 and the two schools came together for a concluding all-day workshop at which each child received a Peer Mediation Certificate. Both schools went on to establish a Peer Mediation Service, with 12 to 15 children functioning as mediators in a rota system. The service operated very effectively during the last two terms of the school year in each school.

Substantial evidence emerged from the pilot project to indicate that the concept of a peer mediation service in primary schools was indeed feasible, given certain conditions. These, significantly, were identified by the Project's new research focus. They related especially to issues often referred to as 'hidden curriculum' issues – ethos, teacher-pupil and whole-school relationships etc. - and pointed to the need for these issues to be unhidden for the sake of an authentic and effective provision of EMU. There had to be congruence between what children were being *taught* about respect for others and how they experienced being treated by adults in the school. It is especially important to have consistency in programmes dealing with relationships and conflict.

QPEP 1988-1994

For QPEP the Peer Mediation Pilot Project constituted both its finale and the launch pad for progressing what it had begun. The EMU Promoting School Project (EMUpsp), the successor of QPEP, was able to 'hit the ground running' with the development and expansion of the Peer Mediation Programme. But before dealing with the legacy a few concluding words are in order about the initiative that was QPEP.

• It had trialled and developed untried strategies of peace education.

• It had provided teachers with ways and means and the confidence and competence to deliver this aspect of EMU more effectively.

• It had, most deservedly, earned the acknowledgement of being totally bipartisan – no mean achievement in the context of the violent inter-communal conflict.

All of these achievements were due especially to Jerry Tyrrell's honest conviction delivered through his skill and leadership.

The Legacy from QPEP

'Although the Ulster Quaker Peace Education Project came to an end in December 1994, the full effect of its influence … is in the legacy it leaves in the form of the EMU Promoting School Project'.

Tyrrell, J. 1995, p.122 T

This was how Jerry concluded his assessment of QPEP, only a few months into the life of the new Project. It is an indication of the enthusiasm and confidence which marked the beginnings of EMUpsp as it set out to grow the Peer Mediation Programme which it had inherited from QPEP in embryonic form. The initial optimism persisted.

141

A recommendation from the QPEP Evaluation, that any future project should seek to employ a teacher on secondment, was realised in the addition to the staff of Brendan Hartop. He came to EMUpsp with years of classroom practice including international experience, and from having been the Primary 7 teacher at

the Model Primary School who had worked with QPEP in the piloting of peer mediation during the 1994/95 school year. (The other schools which participated in the pilot programme were Oakgrove Integrated Primary School in Londonderry, Ballysally Primary School in Coleraine, and St. Theresa's Primary School in Enniskillen). Because previous personnel had limited experience of schools, Brendan had a very substantial impact in terms of the new Project's understanding of and sensitivity to teachers and schools. He reinforced Jerry's emphasis on the importance of affirming teachers for what they were already doing, and being attentive to issues of low morale within the profession. But Brendan went considerably further in challenging the Project to recognise that teachers and schools have a prescribed and packed curriculum to deliver. If what is being proposed is related to the requirements of the curriculum and can provide a way to deliver aspects of the curriculum, then it will interest teachers. Otherwise it may be destined to remain peripheral to the school. Such considerations gelled perfectly with the findings from QPEP about the importance of ethos and whole-school relationships issues in the authentic delivery of EMU.

The new body overseeing EMUpsp was named 'The Positive Ethos Trust'. The professional partnership of Jerry and Brendan led to the development of a peer mediation programme which could belong with integrity at the heart of a school's work in terms of both curriculum and the broad objectives of education. That it was mutually enriching is evidenced by the fact that after Brendan's request for a third year of secondment from his school was refused, he opted to leave the security of permanent employment and stay with EMUpsp. On the strength of his work with EMUpsp he moved into an international engagement with the challenges for education in contested society contexts, in particular in Bosnia Herzegovina and Sri Lanka under the auspices of the UNESCO Centre at the University of Ulster's School of Education. Brendan subsequently became the Centre's Assistant Director.

This author collaborated with Jerry to produce an account of the Peer Mediation Programme's development (Tyrrell & Farrell 1995). EMUpsp was able to facilitate its expansion to State, Controlled and Integrated Primary schools throughout Northern Ireland. Children from all these sectors demonstrated their skills to the Republic of Ireland's President Mary Robinson during a visit to her Residence in September 1996 and EMUpsp contributed regularly to the Annual Conferences of Mediation UK and to other education forums.

Sadly Jerry was struck down with terminal illness while engaged in writing a book on Peer Mediation – bringing the work to a wider audience. Following his death on the 16th December 2001, it was this author's privilege to complete the book and bring it to publication. (Tyrrell 2002).

Following Jerry's death it was decided to locate the work of the Positive Ethos Trust at The Junction – a community relations resource and peace-building centre in Derry established through a partnership between community relations organisations throughout the North West (http://www.thejunction-ni.org). Under its auspices more schools are being provided with training in the delivery of Peer Mediation to their children. The Northern Ireland Council for Integrated Education is currently facilitating the establishment of Peer Mediation, using the EMUpsp resources, in all of the primary schools in the Integrated sector and to other interested schools. This author has facilitated its establishment in a Dublin school and there are possibilities for its significant expansion in the Republic.

CONCLUSION

The purpose of education is to equip children with the values, knowledge and skills they need for their lives, as individuals and as citizens. The fundamental human and global problem is one of relationships, from the interpersonal to the international level and at every level in between. And peace is dependent on people having the confidence, commitment and competence to constructively manage the conflicts that are inevitable in all relationships. In a world where the destructive management of conflicts anywhere poses an ever more serious threat to the well-being and survival of humanity, it is owed as a minimum to children that their education

143

include 'conflict literacy'. Jesus persistently greeted everyone with the word 'shalom'. The word 'peace' fails to convey the richness of the original. A better translation is 'right relationships'. Only when relationships are right can there be real peace. The Quaker Peace Education Project and all that sprang from that Faith-inspired initiative has been powerfully about the promoting of SHALOM among the generations preparing for adulthood.

References

Bernstein, B. (1970) **New Society.** London: IPC Magazines.

Bowers, S. (1984) **Ways and Means – An Approach to Problem Solving:** Kingston Friends Workshop Group, Surrey.

Boyd, F. (1992) **Minutes of Management Committee,** Quaker Peace Education Project (QPEP).

Farrell, S. (1992) **Annual Report 1991/1992,** p.26, QPEP.

Lampen, J. & Farrell, S. (1993) 'The Ulster Quaker Peace Education Project'. In Tattum, D. & Herbert, G. **Countering Bullying: Initiatives by Schools and Local Authorities:** Trentham Books.

Lampen, J. (1993) **Conflict Busters: The Young Peoples' Guide to Mediation in Schools.** QPEP, University of Ulster.

O'Neill, J. (1993) **Final Report. Quaker Peace Education Project. Charities Evaluation Service.** paragraphs 1.3.2, 1.3.4.

Rainey, G. (1993) **Annual Report 1992/1993.** p.55. QPEP.

Smith, A. & Dunn, S. (1990) **Extending Inter-School Links:** University of Ulster, Centre for the Study of Conflict, Coleraine.

The Friendly Word (1986 March/April) 'New Quaker Initiative – Peace Education in Northern Ireland'.

Tyrrell, J. (1988) **Developments in conflict resolution in schools in Northern Ireland.** Forum for Initiatives in Reparation and Mediation Annual Conference, Hoddesdon, Herts.

Tyrrell, J. (1993) **Interview by Jim O'Neill,** QPEP Evaluation.

Tyrrell, J. (1995) **The Quaker Peace Education Project: Developing Untried Strategies.** University of Ulster, Centre for the Study of Conflict, Coleraine. pp.102, 122.

Tyrrell, J. & Farrell, S. (1995) **Peer Mediation in Primary Schools.** University of Ulster, Centre for the Study of Conflict, Coleraine.

Tyrrell, J. (2002) **Peer Mediation: A Process for Primary Schools.** London: Souvenir Press.

Weissglass, J. (1991) "Teachers Have Feelings Too". **Journal of Self-Development.**

Workers Education Association (1988) **Northern Ireland District Guide to Courses.** Autumn Term.

Young, A. (1993) **Annual Report.** Ulster Quaker Peace Education Project 1992/1993.

Chapter 7

IDEAS AND PRACTICES IN SERVICE, DEVELOPMENT AND CONFLICT RESOLUTION

Ann Le Mare

'Only when relationships are right can there
be real peace'
Seamus Farrell (Chapter 6)

THIS CHAPTER will make links between the discussions in the previous chapters and the theories and practices of development, relief work and conflict resolution. The intention is twofold: putting local events and actions into a wider context should help people to learn from their own experiences and, secondly, the work undertaken in Northern Ireland over the last 30 years has relevance beyond this country and will be of interest to people involved in development, service and conflict resolution in other places.

DEVELOPMENT AS CONTEXT

Intentional development activity, sometimes referred to as 'good change' (Chambers 1997), has been an enduring feature of 20th- and 21st-century society (Allen & Thomas 2000), reflecting the desire by individuals and groups to address the shortcomings of different political systems to provide adequate social, cultural, political and economic rights to their citizens. Providing emergency relief and services to people in need has always been one aspect of development work, and indeed, is particularly relevant in situations of communal conflict. Globally, intentional development activity has gone through many different periods, reflecting the dominance of particular political beliefs: for example, state led development programmes were popular in the 60s and 70s, while encouragement of the private sector and market strategies dominated the 80s and a renewed emphasis on civil society groups as the vehicle for development marked the 90s (Willis 2005). Now, moving into the 21st century, a pragmatic approach to development activity dominates, drawing on a range of state, market and voluntary society initiatives as a basis for intervention.

In Northern Ireland development activity has remained loyal to its original approach of community development, adopted in the 70s and a popular strategy in that decade. While the employers have changed from the Northern Ireland Community Relations Commission (NICRC) to community groups, local councils and social services (McCready 2001), the ethos of working directly with and encouraging local level development has endured when it has become less fashionable in other parts of the UK and the world. Professional community development workers played a significant role in consolidating and pursuing a community development strategy, in their networking and sharing of knowledge, in providing reports and evaluations (Deane 1989; CDRG 1990, 1991a, 1991b), and in their continual advocacy on behalf of community groups from across Northern Ireland.

Community Development

Community development was initially envisaged as a radical strategy to address the widespread deprivation in Northern Ireland (Griffiths 1974). It was a response to the view that Northern Ireland was a divided society (Barritt & Carter 1962, Whyte 1990), where the political status of this part of the UK overshadowed attention to the problems shared by both communities. The sharp divide between communities concerned Quakers as 'the constitutional issue was ever to the fore to the neglect of matters of social and economic concern' (Chapman, Chapter 2, p.28). While there is disagreement over the level of alleged discrimination by the state and state institutions (Darby 1976, pp.75-79), it is the case that on 'virtually every indicator of socio-economic disadvantage, Catholics still experience higher levels of need or disadvantage than Protestants' (Darby 1995, p.13). Each community felt threatened by being a minority, the Catholics in the North, and the Protestants in Ireland. This is referred to as the 'double minority model' (Jackson, cited in Whyte 1990, p.100), leading to insecurity and a fear of change with an emphasis on retaining power in whatever sphere possible. Such fears contribute to each community maintaining absolutist positions (Lijphart 1977), a problem often encountered by Quakers.

> '...positive contributions were often undermined by the tendency of politicians and community leaders to reject anything that did not meet their narrowly defined needs.'
>
> (Bennett, Chapter 5, p.103)

A community development approach sought to address insecurity and 'holding onto power' by encouraging a discussion of problems, developing activities that increase social inclusion and fostering integration of different groups into decision making. It focused on self-help, collective action, and the participation of people in their own development (McCready 2001). The philosophy particularly underpinned the approach of CfND (Chapter 4) and contributed to work done by Quaker House (Chapter 5). Working with communities to identify and address their problems inevitably includes working with a range of statutory and voluntary agencies. The request from families visiting relatives in prisoners to have support services led to innovative solutions, such as the first childcare facilities in a prison. Quaker Service sought funding from a range of organisations (Chapter 3), leading to securing additional activities such as counselling and information services and eventually after-care projects.

When working in Northern Ireland, one cannot escape either the violence *within* communities (between rival paramilitary groups), or the violence *between* different communities, ranging from unorganised sporadic bottle throwing and rioting to more 'formal' engagement of paramilitary forces against each other. Community groups could see themselves as an alternative to paramilitary leadership, or be groups that included paramilitary involvement. It should also be remembered that paramilitary organisations saw themselves, and were often viewed by members of the community, as 'a channel for articulating social grievances' (McAuley, cited in Tonge 2002, p.153). The relationships in communities were highly complex, with individuals supporting the use of violence in some situations while arguing against it in other situations. Quaker House maintained contact with various paramilitary members, and at times, provided a means for them to communicate with others (Chapter 5), as well as providing encouragement to adopt alternative methods to achieve their aims.

Initiatives to involve members of paramilitaries in constructive activity laid the foundation for subsequent attempts at the reintegration of ex-combatants. Northern Ireland has been viewed as having some of the most successful reintegration programmes, due to the involvement of ex-combatants in designing and implementing programmes (Rolston 2007), an approach that owes much to the philosophy and experience of community development. In addition, Quakers were active in providing services to support the release of lifers, later transferred to the Northern Ireland Probation Service, and in campaigning for restorative justice programmes (Chapter 3 p.52). Such efforts, along with activities of other organisations, led to many paramilitary members seeking political means to achieve their aims. Members of republican and loyalist groups have shown courage and openness as active participants in the transformation of the conflict (Rolston 2007, p.274), a process of individual change linked, in part, to the concerted effort by a range of individuals and organisations to provide space and opportunities for alternatives to violence. It is also the case that many politicians who were initially opposed to cross-community initiatives showed courage in becoming more involved in inclusive politics.

Community Relations

The other thread that consistently runs through development initiatives in Northern Ireland is a concern for improved community relations with a focus on conflict resolution and reconciliation (Knox 1994, Harvey 1997). The link between religion and politics in Northern Ireland is extensive, more than experienced in other parts of the UK or Ireland. This is due to the direct involvement of churches in political power relations, the widespread social segregation along religious lines, the resources which religious institutions provide and the role of religious ideology in the construction of communal identities (Mitchell 2006, pp.1-2). The NICRC adopted a community development and a community relations focus, encouraging community groups to pursue better relationships with neighbouring communities. All the projects in this book, Quaker Service, Quaker Peace Education, and Quaker House Belfast have examples of working with individuals and groups who wished to respond to the interlocking spirals of deprivation, sectarianism and violence. Another specific example would be the involvement of Friends in the Newry Community Relations Forum.

> *'Important insights were gained, less estrangement is now felt, so that the Forum did strengthen good relations among a diverse group who had a common interest in a better future for Newry.'*
>
> (Chapman, Chapter 2, p.25)

The evaluations of the different Quaker organisations confirm the continued relevance of activities directed at improving relationships between communities where Northern Ireland 'remains a deeply divided society: divided by national and religious identities, by contentious views of history, and by differing aspirations for the future' (Connolly 2006, p.39).

> *'Only when relationships are right can there be real peace.'*
>
> (Farrell, Chapter 6, p.143)

The Quaker Worldview

The ethos of both community development and improved community relations struck a cord with Quaker philosophies, in particular the view that 'there is that of God in every one' and thus, it is not surprising that so many individual Quakers would become involved in organisations that spoke to their testimonies of peace, equality, simplicity and honesty (McCartney, Chapter 1). As Chapter 2 so eloquently relates, 'Friends were not immune from suffering and could identify with the many victims which the Troubles produced' (Chapman, Chapter 2, p.18); facing violence and tensions in their daily lives, such as those who 'refused to pay protection money', and the Friend who 'carried a bomb away from the premises' (Chapman, Chapter 2, p.23).

Thus, the Quaker worldview, 'to respond to where issues of social justice need a voice' (Blair, Chapter 3, p.33) shared many values with the rationale for community development and reconciliation. Often the Quaker organisations allowed their workers an envied freedom to be creative and original, for example in 'identifying and developing untried strategies' (Tyrell, cited in Farrell, Chapter 6, p.127). In addition, Quaker methods were complementary to the ethos of shared activity, and were influential in many of the organisations, for example in the use of consensus for making decisions at CfND and Quaker House 'offering a quiet, non-judgemental space for individuals and groups to explore their own thinking and that of others' (Bennett, Chapter 5, p.116). Another aspect was the close relationship between staff and management committees identified in all four projects.

> '...the role of the committee has been crucial.... ...a mix of experience, contacts and perspectives...this diversity was found useful by the representatives when planning programmes.'
>
> (Bennett, Chapter 5, p.117)

Most of the time such approaches were enabling.

> 'Quakers influenced the ethics and methodology of the organisation in many ways – even down to the importance of keeping good records.'
>
> (Bass, Chapter 4, p.88)

However, there were also situations where Quaker approaches were unhelpful, or limited the ability of some organisations to act.

> 'The use of consensus... did mean that decisions often took a long time... and in some cases may simply have been avoided.'
>
> (Bass, Chapter 4, p.87)

Thus, it was important that these Quaker organisations were 'fit for purpose' (Blair, Chapter 4, p.55), could embark on 'a very steep learning curve' when required (Farrell, Chapter 6, p.134), while being attentive to the wider context, 'The nature of the work at Quaker House itself gradually changed in response to the evolving situation' (Bennett, Chapter 5).

THEMES EMERGING FROM THE QUAKER PROJECTS

The case studies in this book cover a wide range of activities, responding to particular incidents and processes in Northern Ireland at particular times. Stress has been placed on *how* things happened, who was involved, what they did, and some of the outcomes of projects and services. Part of the purpose of this book is to remember, to make sense of a shared history and to learn from our experience, seeing what could be shared more widely across Northern Ireland and indeed to other countries that struggle with similar issues. Important themes that have formed part of the how in the narratives of each organisation have been capacity building, work with other agencies, moves to professionalism, attention to human rights, and issues surrounding sustainability. It is to these themes that we now turn.

Capacity Building

A focus on community development inevitably includes supporting and facilitating educational and training programmes in order to improve the capacities of individuals and organisations to respond to and better their situation. People often cannot participate adequately in society and be involved in decisions that affect their lives, unless they gain increased skills and knowledge, though it is recognised that such processes are complex and often limited by relationships of power and knowledge (Cooke & Kothari 2002). Providing training was an integral part of the ethos of CfND, such as on-the-job training to the neighbourhood workers, trips to Derry, Dublin and other community groups, and sessions on relevant topics (Chapter 4, pp.74-76). While common now, sessions were also arranged for community workers from other agencies, a new venture at that time. The neighbourhood workers, in turn, encouraged training for community members, often as part of new activities in their areas. Another example are the workshops facilitated by QPEP, a significant feature being 'the active involvement of the teachers in planning and delivering of the workshops', where 'teachers acknowledged the relevance of the workshop approach' (Farrell, Chapter 6, pp.6-8). Capacity building at a local and organisational level has been shown to have a link to improving democratic structures within society generally (Williamson 1995; Donaghy 2003). The success of the Civic Forum, and later initiatives such as 'A Shared Future', are in part due to the groundwork laid by many developmental organisations, providing opportunities for people to discuss and articulate their problems, while also learning to listen to the views of others.

Capacity building has also meant building the capacity of the Quaker organisations, and it is significant that each of the organisations invested significant time and energy into research and regular evaluations. In 2002 Quaker House held a workshop with a independent consultant to review progress and redefine their aims (Chapter 5). CfND held an annual conference for staff and committee, setting up working groups around specific issues and inviting speakers to meet with them. An evaluation by an external company was done after 3 years, in 1977, in order to assess the work of the organisation, highlighting positive aspects – the approach to community development worked well and the training programme had been important in developing the effectiveness of the neighbourhood work – as well as things that could be improved – putting more emphasis on influencing agencies and the suggestion to establish local support groups in the neighbourhoods (Chapter 4, p.80). Another example of internal capacity building was when one of the volunteers at Quaker Cottage undertook some research and recommended that 'encouragement be given to the mothers to share in and play with their children at the cottage' (Blair, Chapter 3, p.47), which led to providing not just a place to come, but support and guidance to mothers, leading to changes in behaviour and attitudes.

> *'When I came to Quaker Cottage I thought there was no hope for me…. Now a year on I've changed beyond belief…. I can look to the future now with confidence and that I have one. My children can see a future too….'*
>
> A mother cited in UQSC Annual Report 07/08
> (Chapter 3, p.50)

Advocacy and Engagement with Other Organisations

However, it is not possible for one organisation or local communities to 'go it alone' – they have neither the resources nor the political power to make things happen on their own. In the above example of working with mothers and children, the staff of Quaker Cottage and Quaker Service developed strong links with the Health & Social Services authority, demonstrating how important it is to build vertical and horizontal linkages (Werlin 1992) in order to increase involvement in decision-making and to make institutions accountable. Substantive change at a societal level involves attention to advocacy, networking and engagement with statutory agencies and such links, connecting the micro local level to the macro institutional level, were also part of the work of the organisations discussed in this book. For example, in the above example of working with mothers and their children, the staff at Quaker Cottage and Quaker Service developed a strong link with statutory agencies in order to secure funding and to influence practice more widely.

These processes replicate the themes within conflict resolution, where there is a need to build trust within communities, and between people and organisations, and to alter structures that reproduce the causes of violence. The work undertaken by the Quaker organisations in this book did help to enable links across the society and to encourage shared responsibility for solving problems. Developing such contact and facilitating links between groups is necessary to further the attempts at peace making. Such contacts across society are summarised in Figure 7.1, based on Lederach's theory of conflict transformation where peace needs to be built at different levels, as well as facilitating connections between the different levels.

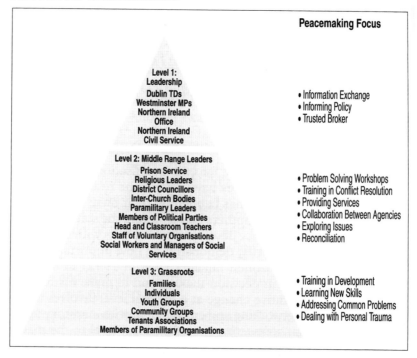

Figure 7.1. Application of Lederach's 3 Levels of Conflict Transformation Applied to Peacemaking in Northern Ireland.

Responding to need sometimes means embarking on new initiatives, such as 'with commendable alacrity and initiative' the decision to set up a summer work camp in Ballymurphy in 1970, where 'with the breakdown of law and order…it was no easy matter to provide a constructive programme' (Chapman, Chapter 2, p.21). Another example is the decision by Quaker Service 'to explore the potential of Restorative Justice as an alternative method within the criminal justice system' (Blair, Chapter 3, p.52), starting with the organisation of a conference, leading to a Restorative Justice Working Group, and making links with community based restorative justice groups. In response to these initiatives, the Northern Ireland Office established a Restorative Justice Steering Group, and the principle of such approaches to juvenile offenders was included in the Justice (NI) Act 2002. At other times, advocacy depends on continuous representation of beliefs and arguments, for example the Ulster Quaker Peace Committee's lobbying of government officials on issues such as 'internment, riot control, the use of torture and plastic bullets' (Chapman, Chapter 2, p.20). The third aspect of advocacy, working with other organisations, is illustrated by the Quaker Peace Education Project, which focused on 'engagement with teachers' and being 'sensitive to the dynamics of schools and the needs of teachers' (Farrell, Chapter 6, p.126).

In addition to working at the community and organisational level, considerable contact was also maintained with politicians, civil servants and those who have influence on policies. Engaging with politicians and policy makers in non-confrontational ways is a significant aspect of resolving conflict and dealing with justified grievances (Lederach 1993, Ross 2000). Such contact was often out of public view, allowing for confidential talks and periods of getting to know other peoples' positions and interests. This work was most consistently encouraged by Quaker House (Chapter 5), but was also supported by the activities of individual Friends (Chapter 2), and by the other organisations when experience suggested the need to present a case to policy makers.

Demands for Professionalism

It is not just other agencies that need to change: it was also found that the organisations that were established and initially managed by Quakers also had to change in response to new situations.

This manifests itself most strongly in the move from volunteerism to professionalism. Both workers and committee members initially were volunteers, giving their time, energy and enthusiasm because they believed in what they were doing, and 'wanted to make a difference'. Increasingly providing individual and family services became more complex and the legislative and legal requirements more onerous on committees. Volunteers felt they needed professional skills, and demands on time and expectations of sophisticated knowledge were growing for voluntary committee members. Thus, staff with professional qualifications and skills came to replace volunteer workers, and committees sought the expertise of professionals such as accountants and solicitors.

'...volunteers were gradually replaced by a number of paid part-time staff. The children's work required qualified workers to meet the stringent requirements of playgroup legislation.'

(Blair, Chapter 3)

These processes mirror the wider world of development, where increased professionalism in development has been driven by demands for improved accountability, choice and financial sustainability (Willis 2005).

Human Rights as a Basis for Development

Human Rights has increasingly become the language of international development and is used to justify global campaigns against injustice, drawing on the Universal Declaration of Human Rights adopted by the United Nations in 1947. A focus on human rights was influential in the adoption of the eight Millennium Development Goals.*

Ideas around human rights were a background to development activity in Northern Ireland. The Civil Rights Movement (CRM), and the reaction to it, is often seen as the start of 'the Troubles' in Northern Ireland. The CRM was an attempt by Catholics, supported by many Protestants, to demand an end to discrimination

---

* The Millennium Development Goals (MDG) is the first time that there has been a global commitment to universal goals, including the reduction of poverty and end of hunger, universal education, gender equality, reduction in child mortality, combating HIV/AIDS, and working towards environmental sustain-ability and global partnerships. www.un.org/millenniumgoals

and reform of government legislation and practices. Attention to civil rights became a significant ideological position among Nationalists. Increasing attention to economic, political, cultural and social rights for all people in Northern Ireland became a foundation for much development activity and to subsequent institutional reform, for example the new Bill of Rights for Northern Ireland (Dixon 2001, p.270). A focus on human rights was also an important aspect of Quaker work, for example, Quaker House (Chapter 5) made a submission to the newly formed Northern Ireland Human Rights Commission. The Commission decided on a policy of placing a 'statutory obligation upon public authorities to promote equal opportunities' (Tonge 2002, p.209). The Quaker Peace Education Project (Chapter 6) worked towards improving the right to have one's culture respected, and through its peer counselling, the social right to a safe and secure environment. CfND (Chapter 4) contributed to people's economic rights through its programmes of local economic development.

However, the achievement of widespread human rights is contested and difficult to implement, not least within Northern Ireland. Conflict between different types of rights is common, for example the right to assembly (the civic right to express one's views) can be in conflict with the right to live without offence (practice of cultural rights) raised by the contested role of Orange Order marches in Northern Ireland (Tonge 2002, p.209). Working to improve human rights for everyone necessitates the ability of people to understand each other, a process facilitated by Friends in many situations, for example, the meetings between Quakers, Unionists groupings, the Orange Order and Republican leaders from the South (Chapter 2, p.26). Quaker House had contact with a range of individuals and organisations involved in sensitive issues around parades (Chapter 5, p.105). Quakers in Northern Ireland can rightly be proud of their contribution to these processes of listening and talking, leading to negotiation and support for shared action.

Sustainability

All of the above themes – capacity building, work with other agencies, professionalism, and attention to human rights – feed into aspects of sustainability. Often sustainability is seen in terms

157

of financial sustainability, the financial security of a particular organisation, and all the Quaker organisations in this book have had to deal with problems of funding. After 15 years, CfND had to close, due to lack of statutory funding, though most of the workers found employment with other agencies. The Quaker House management committee and representatives have spent considerable time in finding continuing and new sources of funding. The valuable work done with teenagers by Quaker Service (Chapter 3, p.51) is in danger of being lost due to a lack of funding. So, funding is a serious problem for voluntary projects.

However, one can also consider sustainability in terms of ideas, of links to policy and of the personal effect on individuals. Many of the programmes and initiatives of these Quaker organisations have been taken up by other organisations, for example the employment of neighbourhood workers by a range of agencies (Chapter 4) and the 'Positive Ethos Trust' now based at 'The Junction' and peer mediation with children now a responsibility of the Northern Ireland Council for Integrated Education (Chapter 6, p.143). Activities have influenced others and initiatives have often led to changes in policy, for example the work done with prisons by Quaker Service, or QPEP emerging as a 'significant contributor to thinking and practice in the field of peace education' (Farrell, Chapter 6, p.129). In addition are the ongoing testimonies of changes in the lives of individuals as a result of contact with the various projects.

> '...the feedback from the women and referrers was overwhelmingly positive, a sign that although the project is small, it is making a significant impact on the lives of those it touches'.
>
> (Bischoff, cited in Chapter 3, p.59)

It is in these very important senses of sustainability – of ideas and change in individuals, rather than permanence of organisations – that Quaker responses to the conflict can be seen as sustainable and enduring.

It has been argued that faith-based work, such as that undertaken by Quakers, cannot be evaluated scientifically, as it is motivated by a particular set of values and beliefs (Yarrow 1978, pp.298-99). However, one can evaluate the methodology, the approaches, and some of the outcomes, that is, the contributions that are made to the wider society. This book is a contribution, then, to the evaluation of faith-based developmental work which has a concern for the resolution of conflicts. It is recognised that such work is complex, with many contributing factors and with a variety of tasks, skills, and interactions that need to be facilitated.

'There is a need to deal with the underlying factors. In a conflict situation these are non-cooperation, deficits in communication, and a lack of self-esteem and appreciation of others. Skills in affirmation, communication and cooperation are central to relationships – and their deficiency is central to conflict'.

(Farrell, Chapter 6, p.129)

One way to think about such complexity is to apply Ross's framework on different approaches to conflict resolution (Figure 7.2, below).

Approaches	Goals	Examples
Community Relations	Improve communication and understanding; promoting tolerance, acceptance of diversity, encouraging structures which safeguard rights of all	Cross community activities and programmes (CfND) Peer Mediation (QPEP)
Principled Negotiation	Positive sum agreements between parties, e.g., ones which provide mutual gain	Parades (Quaker House) Support of community campaigns (CfND)
Human Needs	Shared recognition of core needs and exploration of ways to meet them through joint action	Quaker Cottage, work with young people (Quaker Service) Summer Work Camps (Chapter 2)
Identity	Changed relations through mutual recognition, development of a sense that agreement is possible, lowering fears to permit exploring options	Support to mothers (Quaker Service) Meetings between politicians, and between politicians and paramilitary leaders (Quaker House)
Intercultural Miscommunication	Effective intergroup communication, weakening negative stereotypes	Newry Community Relations Forum (Chapter 2) Joint training programmes (CfND)
Conflict Transformation	Changing relationships and moral growth which produces justice, forgiveness and reconciliation	Restorative Justice (Quaker Service) Workshops in schools (QPEP)

Figure 7.2. Application of Ross's Approaches to Conflict Resolution Applied to Quaker Work in Northern Ireland, Adapted from Ross (2000), Table 1, Major Theories of Practice of Conflict Resolution, pp 1002-23.

Many of the innovative and, at their time, quite radical responses to conflict and deprivation in Northern Ireland have had a lasting impact on individuals and have influenced the policies and practices of a range of other institutions. Programmes have been funded by statutory agencies, taken up in policy and legislation, and new ideas have entered the political sphere for discussion of ways forward. Though a small group of fewer than 800, Quakers in Northern Ireland have made a contribution in providing much needed services, in getting people to think about and act on alternatives to violence and improving communication between different groups, enabling small steps so that bigger ones could be taken in the future (Yarrow 1978).

References

Allen, Tim & Thomas, Alan (2000) **Poverty and Development into the 21st Century.** Oxford: Oxford University Press.

Barritt, Denis & Carter, Charles (1962) **The Northern Ireland Problem: a study in group relations.** Oxford: Oxford University Press.

Chambers, Robert (1997) **Whose Reality Counts? Putting the First Last.** London: Intermediate Technology Publications.

CDRG Community Development Review Group (1990) **Community Development in Northern Ireland: Perspectives for the Future.** Belfast: WEA.

CDRG (1991a) **Community Development in Northern Ireland: Perspectives for the Future.** Belfast: WEA.

CDRG (1991b) **Funding and Support for Community and Voluntary Groups in Northern Ireland.** Belfast: WEA.

Connolly, Christopher (2006) 'Living on the Past: the Role of Truth Commissions in Post-Conflict Societies and the Case Study of Northern Ireland' in **Cornell International Law Journal** 39, pp.401-433.

Cooke, Bill & Kothari, Uma (eds.) (2002) **Participation: the New Tyranny?** London: Zed Books.

Darby (1976) **Conflict in Northern Ireland: the Development of a Polarised Community.** Dublin: Gill & Macmillan; New York: Barnes & Noble.

Darby (1995) **Northern Ireland: Managing Difference.** London: Minority Rights Group International.

Deane, E. (ed.) (1989) **Lost Horizons, New Horizons: Community Development in Northern Ireland.** Belfast: WEA.

Dixon, Paul (2001) **Northern Ireland: The Politics of War and Peace.** Basingstoke: Palgrave.

Donaghy, Tahnya (2003) 'Mainstreaming: Northern Ireland's Participative-Democratic Approach' in **Policies and Politics** 32(1) pp.49-62.

Griffiths, Hywel (1974) **Community Development in Northern Ireland: A Case Study in Agency Conflict. Coleraine:** University of Ulster.

Harvey, Brian (1997) **Report on the Special Support Programme for Peace and Reconciliation.** York: The Joseph Rowntree Charitable Trust.

Knox, C. (1994) 'Conflict Resolution at the Micro Level: Community Relations in Northern Ireland', in **Journal of Conflict Resolution,** 38 (4).

Lederach, John Paul (1993) **Pacifism in Contemporary Conflict: A Christian Perspective.** Paper commissioned by US Institute of Peace and Eastern Mennonite College, International Conciliation Service.

Lijphart, Arend (1977) **Democracy in Plural Societies: A Comparative Exploration.** New Haven (CT): Yale University Press.

McCready, Sam (2001) **Empowering People: Community Development And Conflict,** 1969-1999. Belfast: The Stationery Office.

Mitchell, Claire (2006) **Religion, Identity and Politics in Northern Ireland.** Aldershot: Ashgate.

ODI Overseas Development Institute (1999) **What Can We Do with a Rights-Based Approach to Development?** ODI Briefing Paper 3. London: ODI.

Rolston, B. (2007) 'Demobilization and reintegration of ex-combatants: The Irish case in international perspective' in **Social & Legal Studies** 16 (2) pp.259-280.

Ross, Marc Howard (2000) 'Creating the Conditions for Peacemaking: Theories of Practice in Ethnic Conflict Resolution' in **Ethnic and Racial Studies** 23 (6) pp.10021034.

Tonge, Jonathan (2002) **Northern Ireland: Conflict and Change.** 2nd ed. Harlow: Pearson Longman.

Werlin, H. (1992) 'Linking Decentralization and Centralization: A Critique of New Development Administration' in **Public Administration and Development,** 12. pp

Whyte, J. (1990) **Interpreting Northern Ireland.** Oxford: Clarendon Press.

Willis, Katie (2005) **Theories and Practices of Development.** London: Routledge.

Williamson, A. (ed.) (1995) **Beyond Violence: The Role of Voluntary and Community Action in Building Sustainable Peace in Northern Ireland.** Belfast: Community Relations Council.

Yarrow, C. H. Mike (1978) **Quaker Experiences in International Conciliation.** New Haven and London: Yale University Press.

Chapter 8

CONCLUSIONS – THE SOCIAL WITNESS OF A PECULIAR PEOPLE

Clem McCartney

'a peculiar people, zealous of good works'
Titus 2:15*

I CAN imagine that many readers of the earlier chapters of this book will be struck by how much a small group of Quakers in Ulster has been able to do since the Northern Ireland conflict erupted into open violence. We are told there are less than 800 Quakers in Ulster, somewhat less than 40 years ago, and the work of Quaker bodies described in this book is not the whole story. Arthur Chapman's chapter gives some examples of how individuals and their meetings were involved in other activities, as well as supporting the projects described in other chapters. Some held key positions in social services, culture and the arts, the media, academia and the business world and some rose to high positions in the civil service. How were there enough of them to go around?

They were not of course the only people concerned about the conflict and working to overcome it. This book has concentrated on specifically Quaker work and projects and this chapter also has that focus. There were many much bigger and much more public initiatives which Quakers supported, and there was interaction

---

* Quoted by Robert Barclay, the 17th century Quaker theologian as the Frontispiece of his 'Apology' (Barclay 1678).

and sharing of experience and practice between Quaker and other initiatives, as is mentioned in Chapters 1 and 7. For their own projects they preferred a much more low-key approach. As the quote at the beginning of Chapter 5 says, 'I pin my hopes to quiet processes and small circles, in which vital and transforming events take place' (Jones 1937). No claim is made that they did more than make a small contribution to the overall efforts to resolve the conflict but it may have been a very distinctive and important contribution and it was remarkable that this small group of people could sustain all this work for so long.

It prompts the question of whether there were some intrinsic qualities they had and perhaps still have. Is there something distinctive about Quakers? Does that explain why they could do so much? Quakers do not like to promote themselves and might not like to claim they have special qualities, or that they always live up to their ideals, but Robert Barclay adopted the term 'a peculiar people' – used in the Bible to describe Jews (Exodus 19:5, Deuteronomy 14:2) and Christians (Titus 2.14 and 1 Peter 2.9) – in the sense of a special or distinctive people with their own qualities. It is important to reflect on this question at the end of this book because it can help to identify qualities that are helpful for all good social development.

The apparently pervasive nature of Quaker engagement has to do with circumstances. They were in the right place at the right time. The fact that many of them were in relevant positions has already been noted. The founders of the Centre for Neighbourhood Development were community development officers in the Community Relations Commission and the clerk of Ulster Quaker Service Committee for much of this period has held responsible roles in Social Services management. As well as those mentioned elsewhere in the book, they had the support of significant individuals in relevant positions. Denis Barritt was Secretary of the Belfast Council of Social Welfare (housed incidentally in the former warehouse of a Quaker business family). Belfast Friend Helen Campbell was just retiring from Stranmillis College at the end of the 1960s and offered her skills and expertise in children's play to the work-camps as well as advising and supporting many other organisations working with young children. They helped to see openings and assist projects to prepare themselves for the work.

One can also see that Ulster Friends had some practical advantages. Even though only a few Quakers were working full-time in these projects they were backed up by many others who served as committee members, as volunteers, and local meetings supported all the work financially. The prison canteen claimed at one stage to have volunteers from all the Friends meetings in Northern Ireland and beyond. Like all religious communities in Northern Ireland, Ulster Friends did not all share a common view of the conflict or how it might be resolved but it is noteworthy that in spite of such differences they could all support, albeit at times with reservations, the various forms of Quaker Service. They were also supported by Quakers in Britain and elsewhere. London Yearly Meeting(now BYM) was very supportive and in particular Friends Service Council and its successor bodies, but there was also much support from the United States and elsewhere. There is mention in these chapters of how they provided advice and support and also personnel. 'Quaker' trusts founded by philanthropists such as Rowntree and Cadbury also helped to solve the problem of money. Projects were somewhat more financially secure than in many other agencies.

It is also evident from the experience described in the book that Quakers were well regarded by all sides and seen as impartial and open to everyone. When the workcamp organisers first went to West Belfast and met the local community leader he said that the Quakers were accepted because they had helped people in the famine without attaching any strings. The young organisers were not aware of this but it had been carried down in the historical memory of at least some Catholics that the Quakers offer altruistic help. Another comment was that Quakers were acceptable to all sides because Protestants thought they belonged to their tradition and Catholics knew they did not.

There was also Quaker experience of helping elsewhere in the world, teaching, working in the Friends' Ambulance Unit in the two World Wars, in missionary activities, peace work and political negotiations. Some local Friends had been involved directly and others had been on committees to oversee such work. There is a strong sense of their historical memory which can stimulate the awareness of problems in society, inspire a willingness to act and give the confidence to try to do things often in new and innovative ways.

But all these factors only reinforce the impression that there may have been something about Quakers, perhaps not unique in itself, but significant in the concentration of those qualities in one small group of people. Answering that question may help to identify some qualities that Quakers should hold onto and which others might find helpful. Some of those qualities are explicitly stated in the earlier chapters and others are only implied by the writer. It is referred to in Chapter 3 as the Quaker ethos. At its heart is a form of witness, an expression of faith, as is explained in Chapter 1 and this creates the sense of commitment and purpose which characterizes Quaker engagement with social issues. There is a clue in the fact that the main service organisation of British Friends is called Quaker Peace and Social Witness and the Irish Quaker body which supports development work overseas is called Quaker Faith in Action. These titles are a reminder that for Quakers it is not possible to separate what one believes from what one does. Those beliefs must be expressed in action. If someone needs help, help should be given to the limits of one's ability. Chapter 2 describes how in 1969 Friends gathered together not knowing what they should do, but clear that they had to respond to the situation. In Quaker terms they had a concern which creates the sense of commitment and purpose which has enabled Quakers to be so active and engaged and to make a contribution, often beyond what might be expected.

Furthermore, social witness means that if something is wrong, one cannot be silent and the wrong has to be tackled and so part of Quaker faith in action is a commitment to social justice. Much of the work described in this book was intended to challenge unfairness and inequality and Quakers in their individual capacity played a part in organizations such as the Committee for the Administration of Justice, the main non-governmental organisation dealing with human rights issues. Of course the desires to help and to challenge social injustice do not in themselves ensure that people act wisely and take initiatives which deserve to be remembered. On occasions some Quakers have not been immune to the charge of being naïve and interfering meddlers. But in contrast, the stories told in this book show that the desire to act is often accompanied by attitudes and approaches which are appropriate to the need, because the witness has been guided by core Quaker principles and values and tested through the Quaker method of doing business.

Quaker beliefs and values, developed in a different context and a different time, are very relevant to good social and community work practice, as is explained more fully in Chapter 7. In the projects is seen the expression of the belief that there is that of God in every person, expressed in the encouragement of the founder George Fox: 'then you will come to walk cheerfully over the world, answering that of God in every one'.* This belief encourages Quakers to believe that in all people there are innate qualities of goodness, even though they may not always be evident. It has led Friends to work with people in all kinds of situations, some of whom have been responsible for actions which Friends cannot condone, for example the work in prisons over the last three centuries. The establishment of the Visitors' Centre at Long Kesh followed in that tradition and eventually the workers were able to connect not only with the families but with the prisoners themselves. In that hostile environment they were able to reach out to that goodness in the prisoners and also in the staff and in doing so evoke a response from that aspect of the other person and establish relationships.

The belief of that of God in the other person also encourages respect for that person. In many of the projects the staff are seen standing alongside the other person. It is reported in Chapter 3 that Quaker Cottage is 'a place where mothers find acceptance, love and care – a place to rediscover self-confidence', because this befriending role is an enabling role which allows the other to find and use their own abilities. It also means respecting others' potential and giving them ownership over things that affect them.

This applies not only to those whom Friends were helping but also to partners and colleagues. This was strikingly demonstrated in the Centre for Neighbourhood Development and it was noted that they were one of the first organisations to include staff in the management body and also individuals from the communities with which they were involved. Quaker Peace Education Project also showed this sharing of ownership. The instigator of the project

---

* This phrase is part of a letter written to ministers in 1656 and the full sentence from which this phrase is taken is also apposite in the present context: 'Be patterns, be examples in all countries, places, islands, nations, wherever you come, that your carriage and life may preach among all sorts of people, and to them; then you will come to walk cheerfully over the world, answering that of God in every one'.

stood back from the management body, which in turn facilitated the Director to take responsibility which he shared with volunteer workers, teachers and most importantly the children in the various schools. Often there was a very positive response. Most of the workers in these projects were not Quakers but became very committed to the Quaker ethos. But the writers of these chapters acknowledge that sharing ownership is not always easy and problems arise. But that was never a reason not to believe in this approach.

The sense of that of God in everyone helps to develop the capacity to accept people as they are. The representatives in Quaker House listened without expressing a view. But the people they were talking with would know some of the beliefs that Quakers stand on and those positions would form part of the context of the dialogue even though they might not be expressed directly. Much of the work Friends were involved in could be more effective if they could remain impartial and acceptance of the other as having the potential for good helps to maintain that stance, which makes it easier to understand, if not agree with, the other's motivation. After their service in Quaker House, one pair of representatives wrote a book about Quaker mediation which they called 'Being in the Middle by Being on the Edge' (Williams & Williams 1994) and that title sums up much of the work in this book. By placing their own views and interests on one side, the Quakers found themselves a valued partner and guide to individuals rebuilding their lives and politicians rebuilding the province.

Sometimes Quakers have been accused of standing outside the conflict and not being directly affected by it. It was argued that most of them did not experience what was happening in the communities most affected by the Troubles. But it is clear from this book that many Friends were able to engage as equals with people from all walks of life partly because of the Quaker commitment to simplicity and equality, allowing them to respect people they meet as equals so there is no need for outward show. Early Friends refused to doff their hat as a mark of respect and today Quakers do not need to change their ways to impress others. Quaker House was very modest and simple, much of the furniture second-hand. The representatives offered simple, homemade food, usually vegetarian, but it was nourishing and wholesome. The people who came to Quaker House ranged from Ministers of State to ex-prisoners, but all were received equally even though many of the visitors were accustomed to, and normally expected, luxury and elegance. It was clear that they accepted the Quaker approach and perhaps were influenced by it.

The modesty in outward appearance reflects a modesty about oneself. Quakers are encouraged to believe that they are not in themselves important but a channel for processes to happen and this impressed those with whom they came into contact. They are willing to take a stand for what they believe is right but not for their own self interest or benefit. Nor are they fastidious. They are willing to get their hands dirty and go wherever there is need. They can be very phlegmatic and practical. Chapter 3 points out that in the early days of Quaker Cottage the accommodation was very basic but the workers cheerfully set to work and now there is a fine, purpose-built centre.

Quakers are probably best known for their peace testimony and their commitment to pacifism and non-violence as is explained in Chapter 1. Interestingly, the Ulster Quaker Peace Committee was the group that was described as having at times trouble finding a role. Peace was a dubious concept in Northern Ireland during the Troubles because it was understood to mean accepting peace on the terms of one's opponents, or valuing peace above justice and fairness. From a pacifist perspective there is much more to peace, including respect for the other and finding ways to meet the interests of everyone, but that perspective was often misunderstood by the protagonists in the conflict. It is interesting that Jerry Tyrell at Quaker Peace Education Project did not focus on issues related to the sectarian conflict but everyday issues of conflict in the school and the community. Nevertheless the projects were often a form of peace witness and Friends were clear about their pacifist position and were respected for it. Many of the people with whom they worked were led to rethink their position on violence as a way to resolve conflict.

Supporting the individual's commitment to the values and principles underlying the projects was the structure of the Quaker business method. This relies on finding a common way forward by what they feel is God's leading, rather than making decisions through majority voting. It encourages self awareness and self reflection, encouraging the individual and the group to consider issues in relation to the Quaker values. There are many references to Quaker business methods in this book, and its challenges are not ignored. It is pointed out that it may take a long time to reach decisions and difficult issues can be avoided. It can be bureaucratic. There are references to the amount of paperwork which is produced but those records have been invaluable in writing this book! And by using the Quaker approach to business, the groups were able to maintain a commitment to basic core values while at the same time allowing freedom of choice. The balance between individual action and the corporate framework helped to guide and support those carrying out the day-to-day work.

The emotional burden of this way of working even with the support of a strong committee should not be overlooked. The worker is giving a great deal of him or herself. Two representatives at Quaker House became ill while working there. Other staff in other projects also became drained though perhaps not to the point of becoming ill. Over time the work became more professionalized. It is right that the importance of professional standards should be recognized both for the quality of the service provided and also for the protection of the workers themselves. But there is no evidence that this weakened the core Quaker values that underlie the work.

Overall, Quaker witness has been a potent mix of qualities. Chapter 5 lists some of the ingredients: committed, determined and flexible people; relevant knowledge about the situation and ways to respond; regular reviews and learning from good practice; the quality of staff; and patience because the work is slow and time-consuming. The distinctive Quaker qualities have helped to hold the work together and strengthen the social witness. Ben Pink Dandelion speaking of all the distinctive ways of Quakers, not only in service but also in worship and personal behaviours, argues that these 'peculiarities' were ways of helping the community to remain faithful in earlier centuries (Dandelion 2007, p.62). This has also been the experience of Ulster Quakers in a different context in the last quarter of the 20th century. Not only has their witness and their identity been strengthened by these initiatives but it has brought others to Quakers where they have been able to contribute to the community.

None of these qualities is unique to Quakers. And individual

Friends do not necessarily show these qualities. No special claim is being made for Quakers. But these qualities do show through in the work described in this volume. It does not matter if they are Quaker values or simply the values of good social development practice (see Chapter 7). What does matter is that they have contributed to the work described here and have helped it to be effective and sustained. So the work described and the approach that lies behind it can be commended to those involved in other forms of social development.

References

Barclay, Robert (1678) **An Apology for the True Christian Divinity.**

BYM Britain Yearly Meeting (1994) **Quaker Faith and Practice: The Book of Christian Discipline of the Yearly Meeting of the Religious Society of Friends (Quakers) in Britain.**

Dandelion, Ben Pink (2007) **An Introduction to Quakerism.** Cambridge University Press.

Williams, Steve and Williams, Sue (1994) **Being in the Middle by Being on the Edge: A Quaker Experience of Non-Official Political Mediation.** Sessions of York.

GLOSSARY

ACE – Action for Community Employment – Government job creation scheme.

Alliance Party – Cross-community political party in Northern Ireland.

Anglo-Irish Agreement – Agreement in 1985 between United Kingdom and Republic of Ireland which aimed to bring an end to the Troubles.

Assembly – Northern Ireland legislative assembly in Stormont, Belfast.

AVP – Alternatives to Violence Project.

Belfast Interface Project – Group engaging in development of creative regeneration of Belfast's interface or 'Peace Line' areas.

Bloody Sunday – Name given to 30 January 1972 when British paratroopers shot dead 14 people in Derry at a Civil Rights march.

BYM – Britain Yearly Meeting – Central structure of Religious Society of Friends in Britain.

CCBI – Council of Churches in Britain and Ireland.

CEDI – Community Economic Development Initiative.

CES – Charities Evaluation Service.

CfND – Centre for Neighbourhood Development.

CH – Cultural Heritage.

Churches Peace Education Project – Established in 1978 to support Education for Mutual Understanding (EMU) initiative.

Civil Rights Movement – Campaign for Civil Rights for Roman Catholic minority in Northern Ireland in 1960s and 1970s.

CND – Campaign for Nuclear Disarmament.

Community Dialogue – Organisation which encouraged dialogue about contentious issues in Northern Ireland.

Community Relations Council – Established in 1990 to promote better community relations.

Corrymeela Community – Founded in 1965 as a Christian

Community to promote reconciliation and peace building through healing of social, religious and political divisions in Northern Ireland.

CRIS – Community Relations In Schools.

Derry/Londonderry – Name of city is sensitive – Derry is used more locally as the original name and tends to be used by those with nationalist views. Londonderry was name assigned to city as part of the plantation settlement during 17th century and is used mainly by those with unionist views in Northern Ireland.

Drumcree – Centre of ongoing conflict in Portadown between local Orange Lodges and Catholics or nationalist residents in relation to Orange parade routes.

DUP – Democratic Unionist Party – Founded and led by Reverend Ian Paisley and presently sharing power with Sinn Fein in Northern Ireland Assembly.

ECONI – Evangelical Contribution On Northern Ireland – now Centre for Contemporary Christianity.

Embrace – Christian Group working to promote a positive response to racial issues in Northern Ireland.

EMU – Education for Mutual Understanding.

EMUpsp – EMU Promoting Schools Project.

ENCORE – European Network for Conflict Resolution in Education.

Fellowship of Reconciliation (FOR) – Largest and oldest international interfaith peace organisation in USA and internationally.

Friends Institute – Part of Frederick Street Meeting House Belfast – Originally used for adult education and now used by Concern (a Third World Charity).

Friends Service Council – Service organisation set up jointly by Britain (then London) and Ireland Yearly Meetings, based in London. Later called Quaker Peace and Service and now called Quaker Peace and Social Witness.

FWCC – Friends World Committee for Consultation – World body of Quakers.

Good Friday Agreement – Political deal reached in Belfast in

1998 – Led to formation of new Northern Ireland Assembly.

Holiday Projects West – Established in 1972 in Derry to send groups of Catholic and Protestant Children on holiday to provide respite during the Troubles.

ICC – Irish Council of Churches – Established in 1923 to bring non-Catholic churches together. INLA – Irish National Liberation Army - small left wing Republican splinter group.

INNATE – Irish Network for Nonviolent Action, Training and Education. Integrated Education – Schools where children of Catholic, Protestant and all faiths are educated together. Schools were first established in 1980s.

IRA – Irish Republican Army. There are several bodies calling themselves IRA. The largest of these is the Provisional IRA, also known as the RA.

Ireland Fund – Registered in USA as an international charity which has raised large amounts of money to support peace building in Northern Ireland.

Irish Young Friends Committee – Group which arranges activities for young Irish Friends.

Irish Young Friends Quarterly – Journal for younger Irish Friends no longer published.

IYM – Ireland Yearly Meeting of Religious Society of Friends.

Jessie Cairns Bequest – An Ulster Quaker legacy.

JPEP – Joint Peace Education Programme of the Irish Council of Churches and Irish Commission for Justice and Peace

LEDU – Local Enterprise Development Unit – a Government body.

Londonderry/Derry – Name of city is sensitive – Derry is used more locally as the original name and tends to be used by those with nationalist views. Londonderry was name assigned to city as part of the plantation settlement during 17th century and is used mainly by those with unionist views in Northern Ireland.

Loyalist – Extreme Unionist.

Loyalist Military Command – Umbrella body for Loyalist paramilitary groups in Northern Ireland set up in 1990s.

Mediation Northern Ireland – NGO set up in 1991 to work with people affected by conflict division and violence – previously known as Mediation Network.

Nationalist – Someone sympathetic to the reunification of Ireland. Usually Catholic.

National H-Block Committee – Pressure group campaigning on behalf of political status for Republican Prisoners. H Blocks – Prison design H shaped high security blocks.

New Ireland Forum – Political group led by Garret FitzGerald (Leader of Fine Gael Party in Republic of Ireland) in 1983 to discuss ways of bringing peace and stability to the whole of Ireland.

New Ireland Movement – Political movement founded in 1969 by Brian Walker, a Friend.

NGO – Non Governmental Organisation.

NICRA – Northern Ireland Civil Rights Association.

NICRC – Northern Ireland Community Relations Commission established in 1969 to foster harmonious relations in Northern Ireland and abolished in 1974.

NIO – Northern Ireland Office – British Department that governs Northern Ireland.

NIVT – Northern Ireland Voluntary Trust – now known as Community Foundation for Northern Ireland.

Northern Friends Peace Board – Peace body in North of England.

Northern Ireland Committee – Ireland Watching Committee – bodies of knowledgeable Quakers from Britain and Ireland North and South who oversaw early work of Quaker Peace Representatives in Frederick Street and Quaker House.

Northern Ireland Trust for Integrated Education – Brings Children from both Roman Catholic and Protestant Faiths to be educated together.

Orange Order – Members are exclusively Protestant and hold annual parades throughout Northern Ireland on 12th July.

PACE – Protestant And Catholic Encounter – Voluntary group bringing both groups together for joint purposes.

Parades Commission – Government organisation set up in 1998 which reviews and makes recommendations about street parades in Northern Ireland.

Pax Christi – International Catholic peace movement.

Peace Line – Wall built in Belfast to separate Protestant and Catholic communities.

Peace People – Founded in 1976 by Mairead Corrigan Maguire, Betty Williams and Ciaran McKeown as a protest movement against ongoing violence in Northern Ireland.

Peace Train Campaign – Set up in 1980s as a response to IRA efforts to disrupt Belfast-Dublin rail link. Members travelled on specially chartered trains.

PRG – Peace and Reconciliation Group – Offshoot of Peace People in Derry.

PUP – Progressive Unionist Party linked to UVF (Ulster Volunteer Force) paramilitary group.

PSNI – Police Service of Northern Ireland. QCEA – Quaker Council of European Affairs – NGO at European Union.

QPEP – Quaker Peace Education Project.

QPS – Quaker Peace and Service – now known as QPSW – Quaker Peace and Social Witness and based In London.

QHB – Quaker House Belfast – often called Quaker House in this book – not to be confused with Quaker House Dublin, where Ireland Yearly Meeting is based.

Quaker Cottage – Family-focused project run by Quaker Service.

Quaker Service – Previously known as Ulster Quaker Service Committee until 2007.

Quaker Tapestry – The Quaker Tapestry is a modern embroidery of 77 fascinating panels. Made by 4,000 men, women and children, this international community project explores three centuries of social history. The Exhibition Centre in Kendal, Cumbria, UK is open to the public from early spring to late autumn each year. For more information visit their website www.quaker-tapestry.co.uk

QUNO – Quaker United Nations Office located in Geneva and New York.

QWC – Quaker Work Camps, now Quaker Social Action

Republican – Avid proponent of a United Ireland, includes members of Sinn Fein.

Relatives for Justice – Organisation providing support for victims and survivors of Northern Ireland, mainly state, violence.

Religious Society of Friends – Formal name for Quakers.

RUC – Royal Ulster Constabulary – replaced by Police Service of Northern Ireland in 2001.

SAS – Special Air Services –Under cover unit of British Army.

SDLP – Social Democratic and Labour Party – a Nationalist political party.

Sinn Fein – Irish Republican political party presently sharing power in Northern Ireland Assembly with DUP.

Special Category Prisoners – Prisoners remanded and/or sentenced for politically motivated offences.

Sunningdale Agreement – 1974 agreement that provided sharing political power between Unionists and Nationalists and a role for Government of Republic of Ireland.

The Friendly Word – Ireland's bi-monthly Quaker journal.

The Junction – Cross-Community Centre for Voluntary Groups in Derry.

The Troubles – Local name given to period of political unrest and violence in Northern Ireland during 1970s, '80s, and '90s.

UDA – Ulster Defence Association – Largest Loyalist paramilitary group.

Ulster Quarterly Meeting – Quaker regional structure in Ulster.

Ulster Workers Council – Loyalist workers organisation set up in 1974 which held a general strike in protest against the Sunningdale Agreement.

Unionist – Supporter of political link between Northern Ireland and Great Britain.

UQPC – Ulster Quaker Peace Committee – a committee of Ulster Quarterly Meeting.

UQSC – Ulster Quaker Service Committee – now known as Quaker Service.

UUP – Ulster Unionist Party – Traditionally largest Unionist political party in Northern Ireland, now smaller than DUP.

UVF – Ulster Volunteer Force – a paramilitary group linked to

PUP (Progressive Unionist Party). VSB – Voluntary Service Bureau – a volunteer organisation based in Belfast.

WEA – Workers Educational Association, an adult education body

West Midlands Quaker Peace Education Project – an English Peace Group. Women in Faith – Non-denominational peace group formed by Lady Mayhew during 1980s.

Appendix 1

EXTRACT FROM DECLARATION OF FRIENDS HISTORIC PEACE TESTIMONY

We utterly deny all outward wars and strife, and fightings with outward weapons, for any end, or under any pretence whatever: this is our testimony to the whole world. The Spirit of Christ by which we are guided is not changeable, so as once to command us from anything as evil, and again to move unto it; and we certainly know, and testify to the world, that the Spirit of Christ, which leads us into all truths, will never move us to fight and war against any man with outward weapons, neither for the kingdom of Christ, nor for the kingdoms of this world.

From *A Declaration from the Harmless and Innocent People of God, called the Quakers,* presented to Charles II, 1660

Quoted in *Christian Experience,* Ireland Yearly Meeting 1962

CHRONOLOGY OF EVENTS IN NORTHERN IRELAND

1919-21: Irish war of independence from British rule.

1922: Agreement between Irish rebels and British sees independence for twenty-six counties of Ireland. The remaining six counties form Northern Ireland, which has a majority Protestant Unionist population and remains under British rule.

1922-68: Sporadic sectarian violence in Northern Ireland which remains under the tight grip of the majority Protestant Unionists.

1968: The Northern Ireland Civil Rights Association starts a campaign to demand equal rights for Catholics who are discriminated against in housing, employment and political representation.

1969: British troops arrive in Northern Ireland, initially to stop violence against the Civil Rights marchers by militant Protestants who fear they are a front for the Irish Republican Army (IRA). Sectarian violence, known locally as the Troubles, breaks out with rioting mainly in Belfast and Derry in August. The Northern Ireland Community Relations Act establishes the Ministry of Community Relations and the Northern Ireland Community Relations Commission.

First meeting of the Belfast Friends Emergency Committee takes place.

1970: Provisional IRA is formed following a split in the IRA. Northern Ireland Community Relations Commission is set up.

First Irish Quaker Workcamps playscheme takes place in Ballymurphy.

1971: The British government introduces internment in August. Most internees were Catholics. Official and Provisional IRA attacks increase.

1972: The worst year of the Troubles begins with 'Bloody Sunday' in which the British Army shoots dead 14 civilians in Derry. The Official IRA blows up the Aldershot barracks of the regiment responsible and kills cleaners and clergy. The Officials declare a ceasefire which is not rescinded. The Provisional IRA carries out hundreds of bombings and shootings. The most notorious was 'Bloody Friday' in which 22 bombs were detonated in one hour in Belfast, killing nine civilians.

Direct rule from Westminster is introduced following the resignation of the Northern Ireland Government. The right to trial by jury for certain paramilitary offences is removed with the introduction of Diplock courts.

Ulster Quaker Service Committee is formalised and starts work at Long Kesh Prison.

1973: Elections to a new Northern Ireland Assembly are held and in December the Sunningdale Agreement sets up the first Unionist-Nationalist (Protestant-Catholic) power-sharing executive.

1974: The Executive is brought down after Loyalists, alarmed at the Irish Republic's role in the settlement, launch a general strike in May. The UVF explodes bombs in Dublin and Monaghan and there are IRA bombings in London, Guildford and Birmingham. The Northern Ireland Community Relations Commission is wound up.

1975: The Provisional IRA announces a ceasefire which broke down a year later. Internment is ended.

Centre for Neighbourhood Development starts work.

1976-7: Peace People Initiative mobilises citizens against violence but does not maintain momentum. Labour government pursues Ulsterisation and criminalisation policies, treating paramilitaries as common criminals and using the RUC where possible to deal with security.

1979: Irish National Liberation Army (INLA) murders Shadow Northern Ireland Secretary, Airey Neave, with a car bomb at the House of Commons. The IRA kills Lord Mountbatten and 18 British soldiers in a single day.

1980: First IRA/INLA hunger strike starts in October and is called off in December.

1981: IRA and INLA prisoners renew their hunger strike in support of special-category status for prisoners, resulting in the death of 10 Republicans. One of the prisoners, Bobby Sands, is elected as an MP. After his death his election agent is elected. Sinn Fein begins its 'armalite and ballot box' strategy.

Lagan College, the first integrated school in Northern Ireland opens.

1982: Elections to Northern Ireland Assembly are held in October and the Assembly meets for the first time in November although Sinn Fein and SDLP members do not take their seats.

Quaker House is established.

1983: New Ireland Forum is established. Department for Education introduces the Education for Mutual Understanding (EMU) projects in schools.

Quaker Peace Education Project is established.

1984: Provisional IRA carries out bomb attack on Conservative Party Conference in Brighton.

1985: Anglo-Irish Agreement is signed between Irish and British governments. The Irish government is to gain an advisory role on Northern Ireland, which is confirmed as a part of the United Kingdom unless a majority votes for reunification. Both sides in Northern Ireland reject it and Unionist MPs resign from Westminster.

1986: Northern Ireland Assembly is abolished.

1987: The SAS kills eight Provisional IRA members at Loughall. The IRA bombs a Remembrance Day parade in Enniskillen, killing eleven.

Statutory support for cross-community schools projects is initiated. Northern Ireland Conflict Mediation Association (later Northern Ireland Mediation Network) is formed.

1989: International Fund for Ireland is set up as a channel for US and international funds.

1990: Northern Ireland Secretary of State, Peter Brooke, declares that Britain has 'no selfish strategic or economic interest in Northern Ireland'.

Northern Ireland Community Relations Council is established.

1992: *Centre for Neighbourhood Development closes.*

1993: A series of atrocities, including IRA bombs in Warrington killing two children and in the mainly loyalist Shankill killing nine, with Loyalist paramilitary responses, do not prevent political movement. The Downing Street Declaration is issued by John Major and the Irish Taoiseach, Albert Reynolds, on 15 December. It confirms that there is to be no change in the constitutional status of Northern Ireland without the consent of the majority. The future of Ireland should be self-determined by the Irish people on a North and South basis.

1994: Downing Street Declaration confirms Northern Ireland's right to self-determination, but adds that the people of the whole island have the right to solve problems on the island without interference from outside. Ian Paisley, leader of the Democratic Unionist Party (DUP), rejects it as a 'sell-out'.

IRA calls a 'complete cessation of operations'. Loyalist paramilitaries reciprocate six weeks later.

1995: Framework Documents are issued, calling for a devolved Northern Ireland Assembly and cross-border political and economic bodies.

1996: Mitchell Commission proposes decommissioning of paramilitary weapons in parallel with all-party talks. The British government calls elections to a 'Peace Forum'. The IRA resumes violence, as a bomb at Canary Wharf kills two. Sinn Fein is excluded from multi-party peace talks. Largest bomb to be planted in England is exploded by the IRA in Manchester.

The RUC blocks the annual Orange Order march at Drumcree, Portadown in July resulting in widespread unrest in loyalist areas. Trouble breaks out over this issue every July for several years.

1998: Belfast or Good Friday Agreement signed between British and Irish governments with the aim of restoring a devolved power-sharing executive in Belfast. Ireland drops its territorial claim to Northern Ireland after an overwhelming majority endorses the agreement in referenda north and south of the border. Newly-elected assembly meets on July 1. The Parades Commission is set up.

A splinter Republican group, the Real IRA, explodes a massive bomb in Omagh.

1999: First power-sharing executive is formed with David Trimble, leader of the Ulster Unionist Party (UUP), as First Minister.

2000: New Assembly is suspended because of lack of progress over decommissioning but is reinstated later in the year. Saville Inquiry into Bloody Sunday begins.

2001: RUC is replaced by the Police Service of Northern Ireland (PSNI).

2002: Power-sharing executive is suspended after Unionists walk out when police investigate Sinn Fein members on allegations of spying for the IRA within the assembly's Stormont building.

2004: Political deal unravels in December over photos of IRA arms, indicating that the paramilitary group had not decommissioned its weapons as agreed.

2005: The IRA formally orders an end to its armed campaign.

The International Monitoring Commission (IMC) says it is satisfied that the IRA has decommissioned its arms. Court proceedings against three men accused of spying for the IRA at Stormont are dropped.

2006

April 6: Prime Ministers Tony Blair of Britain and Bertie Ahern of Ireland announce November 24 as deadline for Northern Ireland Assembly members to set up power-sharing executive.

May 15: Stormont Assembly sits for first time since suspension in 2002.

Oct 11: Multi-party talks begin in St. Andrews, Scotland to broker a deal to restore devolution.

Nov 24: A transitional assembly is installed.

2007

Jan 28: Sinn Fein members vote to support the Police Service of Northern Ireland for the first time, a decision seen as essential for the restoration of power-sharing.

Mar 7: Elections to Northern Ireland Assembly. The DUP and Sinn Fein emerge as the largest parties.

Mar 29: *Ulster Quaker Service Committee becomes Quaker Service.*

May 8: Northern Ireland Assembly reconvenes. Direct rule over Northern Ireland by Westminster officially ends after almost five years. DUP leader Ian Paisley and Sinn Fein's Martin McGuinness are sworn in as First and Deputy First Ministers.